RICH BUNDSCHUH & TOM FINLEY

M·I·C·R·O
MESSAGES

FOR JUNIOR HIGH AND HIGH SCHOOL MINISTRIES

30 Complete One-Page Messages Plus a Reproducible Bible Tract for Every Lesson!

Gospel Light

Gospel Light is an evangelical Christian publisher dedicated to serving the local church. We believe God's vision for Gospel Light is to provide church leaders with biblical, user-friendly materials that will help them evangelize, disciple and minister to children, youth and families.

We hope this Gospel Light resource will help you discover biblical truth for your own life and help you minister to youth. God bless you in your work.

For a free catalog of resources from Gospel Light please contact your Christian supplier or call 1-800-4-GOSPEL.

PUBLISHING STAFF
Jean Daly, Editor
Kyle Duncan, Editorial Director
Gary S. Greig, Ph.D., Vice President, Editor in Chief
Mario Ricketts, Designer

ISBN #0-8307-1578-9
© 1995 Gospel Light Publications
All rights reserved.
Printed in U.S.A.

How to Make Clean Copies from This Book

YOU MAY MAKE COPIES OF PORTIONS OF THIS BOOK WITH A CLEAN CONSCIENCE IF:

- you (or someone in your organization) are the original purchaser;
- you are using the copies you make for a noncommercial purpose (such as teaching or promoting your ministry) within your church or organization;
- you follow the instructions provided in this book.

HOWEVER, IT IS ILLEGAL FOR YOU TO MAKE COPIES IF:

- you are using the material to promote, advertise or sell a product or service other than for ministry fund-raising;
- you are using the material in or on a product for sale;
- you or your organization are **not** the original purchaser of this book.

By following these guidelines you help us keep our products affordable.

Thank you,

Gospel Light

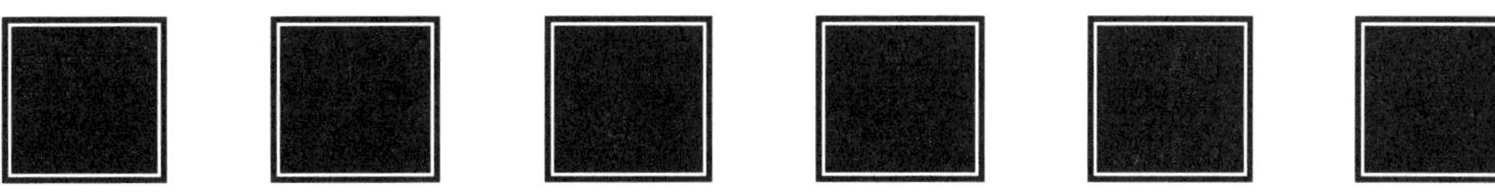

Contents

What Is a Micro Message?

Tear one of the cartoon pages from this book, slap it on your church photocopier, make a ton of copies, then cut, fold and staple as directed and there you have it—a Micro Message! It's a cartoon story in booklet form that will have your students reading and talking; it's a great way to start meaningful discussions about issues of concern to kids.

There are 30 Micro Messages in all, each designed to communicate biblical truth to the young people you work with. Want to teach about the power of the Holy Spirit? Try "Power to Spare" or "What Mason Saw." Do your charges need to consider their language? Show them "The Story of Foul Mouth Mary" and see what they say!

And Micro Messages come in two exciting flavors! Use them to build a terrific Bible study with the help of the simple but complete teaching plan that comes with each. Or, give away Micro Messages alone as simple booklets with quick but powerful messages. Either way, you have 30 wonderful ways to communicate God's truth in a language young people love.

How to Use *Micro Messages*

Each of the 30 chapters in this book features three items: A one-page Bible lesson plan, the two-page reproducible cartoon story and a reduced version of the cartoon that can be easily read. (Because it is to be cut and folded, the actual reproducible cartoon does not follow a beginning-to-end pattern.)

1. The Bible Teaching Plan

Want to use Micro Messages in Sunday School or at any youth meeting? Use the supplied Bible teaching plans. Each plan features simple but effective teaching methods and ideas that will fill an hour with solid Bible learning. The plans tell you everything you need to know; they include materials required for learning activities, discussion questions based on the Scriptures studied, life application activities and information on when and how to use the cartoon booklets.

2. The Reproducible Cartoon Story

There's a nice thing about the Micro Message cartoons—they are reproducible. You can crank out as many as you like! Got 6 kids in your group...or 60? Make as many copies as you need. And don't forget to make a bunch for your kids to give to their friends! For complete instructions, see the article "Making and Assembling Micro Messages is Easy and Fun!"

3. The Reduced Version of the Cartoon Story

This one-page version of the cartoon story is here simply to let you quickly read the story. The cartoon panels are arranged in order so you can read from beginning to end without having to stand on your head.

Put them all together and you've got a winner! Thanks for purchasing *Micro Messages*. We know you will be able to put it to good use for the furthering of God's kingdom on earth.

Making and Assembling Micro Messages is Easy and Fun!

Make it a party! Get your students, some assembly tables and lots of party snacks. Even a few kids can turn out hundreds of booklets an hour.

1. Each cartoon story is on two pages. To begin, remove your favorite cartoon original from this book. The back page of most of the cartoon stories has a blank space—great for phone numbers, church addresses and meeting info.

2. Follow the instructions for making duplex copies on your copy machine. Make the copies back-to-back on letter-size paper just like the original. Make as many as you like. Bright-colored paper gives extra punch.

3. Cut the copies into three equal pieces as shown. A paper cutter is the best method. The more accurate you cut and fold, the better the finished product will be.

4. Assemble the three pieces in the correct order. The page numbers will help you keep everything in proper order.

5. Fold and staple each booklet. One staple per book ought to do it. And there you have it!

Let Us Know What You Think

We'd love to hear about your classroom experiences. And if you have any ideas for subjects you'd like to see covered, send them along, too. You can write to the authors at:
Gospel Light Publications
2300 Knoll Drive
Ventura, CA 93003

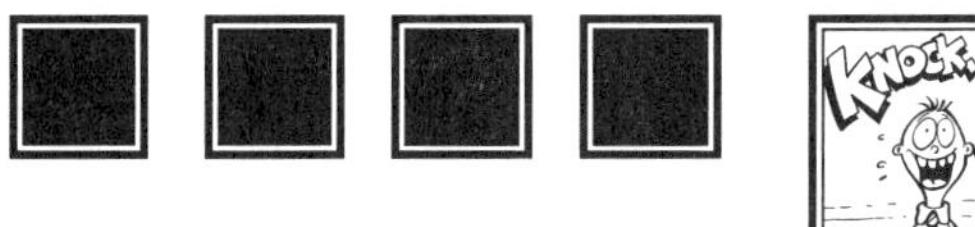

Knock, Knock

Focus of the Lesson: Christians must be cautious about counterfeit brands of Christianity.
Biblical Basis: Matthew 24:4,24; 1 Timothy 6:3-5; 1 John 4:1-3; Jude 4
Materials Needed: Copies of the "Knock, Knock" booklet, paper, felt-tip pens, pencils, paper, a piece of currency, play money.

Step 1—Approach to the Word

Pass around a real piece of currency (make it a low denomination if you have the kind of students who will try to pocket it) and pass around some play money (like Monopoly money). Say to your students, **I sent around two types of money. Obviously, if I tried to pay you for mowing the lawn with the play money you would say, "No way!" You can tell quickly the genuine from the fake. But, if I was truly trying to pass you a counterfeit bill, what would I have to do to convince you? How do countries safeguard their currencies against fakers? How would you know if you got your hands on fake money? Transition to the lesson by saying, Today we are going to look at religions that try to pass themselves off as Christian. They do so by copying many of the things that are distinct in true Christianity, but we can tell the difference! Let's find out how!**

Step 2—Exploration of the Word

Have your class form groups of three or four students. Pass out paper and felt-tip pens to each group and ask them to read the following passages: Matthew 24:4,24; 1 Timothy 6:3-5; 1 John 4:1-3; Jude 4. Have students create warning posters that the Early Church leaders might have posted in their churches to warn the people of the false teachers and counterfeiters of the faith that were coming in. Share and hang up posters.

Step 3—Life Exploration

Pass out copies of the "Knock, Knock" booklet to your group. Ask them to read it over and to write down on a sheet of paper what they think makes these guys a religious counterfeit of true Christianity. They probably will come up with at least some of these things: They claim to have new truth or a corner on truth; they deny important doctrines such as hell, the Trinity, justification by faith in Christ. Point out that the thing that makes a group fake or a cult is not a particular custom, dress or even an activity (like going door-to-door) but a departure from important foundational truths of God. Be prepared to explain the fundamental beliefs of the Christian faith to your students if they are not familiar with them.

Step 4—Conclusion

Discuss with your group what they should do in order to know the difference between true Christian groups and counterfeit ones. Ask, **How could a person your age begin to prepare him- or herself for knowing which groups are valid and which are fake?** After your students have given their ideas, suggest that the best way to know what is phony is to know what is true! Challenge your students to read their Bibles every day during the next week in order to be better acquainted with genuine truth. You may wish to pass out slips of paper and ask your students to write notes of commitment between themselves and God. Have them take their notes and post them in their rooms where they can be reminded about their commitments. Close in prayer.

NOT EVERYTHING THAT SEEMS GENUINE REALLY IS! SPIRITUAL COUNTERFEITS ABOUND. BE WARY OF ANYONE SUGGESTING THAT HIS OR HER GROUP HAS THE INSIDE SCOOP ON TRUTH! KNOW WHAT YOU BELIEVE AND WHY YOU BELIEVE IT! WITH ALL THE FAKE AND PHONY SPINOFFS OF CHRISTIANITY AROUND, THE ADVICE OF THE BIBLE IS WELL TO BE HEEDED. "LET NO ONE DECEIVE YOU WITH EMPTY WORDS" (EPHESIANS 5:6).

NOT EVERYTHING THAT SEEMS GENUINE REALLY IS! SPIRITUAL COUNTERFEITS ABOUND. BE WARY OF ANYONE SUGGESTING THAT HIS OR HER GROUP HAS THE INSIDE SCOOP ON TRUTH! KNOW WHAT YOU BELIEVE AND WHY YOU BELIEVE IT! WITH ALL THE FAKE AND PHONY SPINOFFS OF CHRISTIANITY AROUND, THE ADVICE OF THE BIBLE IS WELL TO BE HEEDED. "LET NO ONE DECEIVE YOU WITH EMPTY WORDS" (EPHESIANS 5:6).

KNOCK KNOCK
RICK BUNDSCHUH

SLAM!

AND WE'D LIKE TO SHARE WITH YOU A FEW OF OUR MATERIALS IN WHICH YOU'LL FIND OUR ALL NEW AND IMPROVED VERSION OF GOD'S WORD !!
FAKE
FORGED
LIES
MORE LIES
BOGUS NEWS
PULL THE OTHER ONE
½ TRUTH

YOU CAN HAVE THE FUN OF LETTING OUR GROUP TELL YOU WHAT THE BIBLE REALLY SAYS... AND SAVE YOURSELF THE TROUBLE AND HASSLE OF HAVING TO STUDY IT YOURSELF.

YOU SEE, WE HAVE DISCOVERED THAT ALL OF THOSE DIFFICULT AND UNPLEASANT IDEAS ... HELL, THE TRINITY, SALVATION BY FAITH ... ARE REALLY UNTRUE !

HI! WE'RE FROM THE ONLY CHURCH WITH AN EXCLUSIVE INSIDE CORNER ON SPIRITUAL TRUTH!
I'VE GOT A BRIEFCASE TOO!
ACME OFFICIAL CULT BRIEFCASE

2

YOU KNOW, I THINK YOU SHOULD DROP THE BIT ABOUT THE TIE, IT ALWAYS SEEMS TO TURN THEM OFF TO OUR PITCH
YEAH? I THINK IT'S PROBABLY YOUR QUIP ABOUT NAME TAGS AND BRIEFCASES THAT DOES IT!

11

WHAT? YOU THOUGHT GOD WAS CHANGELESS? UH..UM... OH, HE IS! ...BUT IT TOOK OUR GROUP TO DISCOVER WHAT IT WAS THAT HE NEVER CHANGED TO!
NICE DOUBLE-SPEAK, RALPH!

4

AND ONCE YOU REALLY BUY INTO ALL OF OUR NONSENSE, YOU CAN GO DOOR-TO-DOOR WITH US ... AND BEST OF ALL... YOU GET TO WEAR A TIE!
OR EVEN HAVE A NAME TAG OR BRIEFCASE... COOL!!
EARL

9

IN FACT, IF YOU JOIN US, YOU CAN TRY TO GET SALVATION BY YOUR OWN EFFORT AND GOOD DEEDS... YOU KNOW, EARN IT... THE AMERICAN WAY!!

6

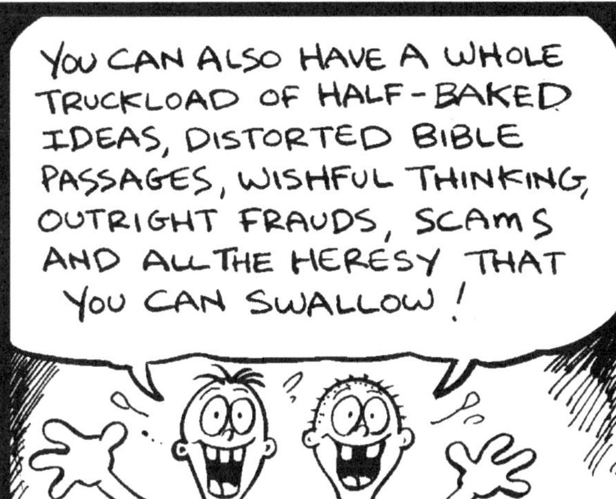

YOU CAN ALSO HAVE A WHOLE TRUCKLOAD OF HALF-BAKED IDEAS, DISTORTED BIBLE PASSAGES, WISHFUL THINKING, OUTRIGHT FRAUDS, SCAMS AND ALL THE HERESY THAT YOU CAN SWALLOW!

7

The Story of Foul Mouth Mary

Focus of the Lesson: A changed heart means a changed life.
Biblical Basis: Luke 6:43-45
Materials Needed: Copies of "The Story of Foul Mouth Mary" booklet, paper, pencils, chalkboard and chalk or overhead. Optional: a large paper heart.

Step 1—Approach to the Word

Distribute copies of "The Story of Foul Mouth Mary" booklet to your students. Ask them to read *only* to page five of the booklet. Then ask, **How many of you know someone who fits the description of Foul Mouth Mary? Why do you think people use such foul language?**

Vote on which reason given in the first five pages of the booklet is the most plausible for people using foul language: 1. Don't know any other words to use; 2. Copied the speech used in movies and recordings; 3. Learned from parents; 4. Imitated friends.

Transition to the lesson by saying, **While there is no doubt that many people have language that is influenced by those around them, let's read the rest of the booklet and see if there might be a deeper reason for this and any other kind of offensive talk.**

Step 2—Bible Exploration

Divide your students in groups of four to six students. Ask each group to read Luke 6:43-45 and then rewrite the main idea of the passage in a poetic form or as a jingle to a commercial tune. Ask your groups to share what they have created.

Step 3—Life Exploration

On a chalkboard or overhead create two columns. At the top of one write the word "Polluted" and at the top of the other column write "Clean." Ask your students to contribute ideas as to what kind of speech might belong in each column. At first students may play it safe and put swearing in one column and praise in another. Prod their thinking by asking them to decide where to put speech such as put-downs, jokes, sarcasm, teasing, white lies, criticism, gossip, complaining and scolding. Ask if there might be conditions where those are good rather than bad. Emphasize the idea that if the heart is pure, the natural result will be speech that is aimed for the good of others, even in joking and teasing. It is not our behaviors that need the work—it's our hearts.

Discuss how one goes about changing the condition of one's heart.

Step 4—Conclusion

Ask your students to commit to spending a few minutes each day this week to recheck their "heart conditions." You may want to create a large heart and hang it on the wall. Have those students who would be willing to spend a minimum of two minutes each day examining their inner lives write their names on the heart as a pledge of commitment.

THE STORY OF
FOUL
#@!$%*
MOUTH MARY
RICK BUNDSCHUH

ONCE UPON A TIME THERE WAS A YOUNG LADY WHOSE LANGUAGE COULD PEEL THE PAINT FROM A FENCE. HER NAME WAS "FOUL MOUTH MARY."
*!!$ %$@ #?<>

SOME THOUGHT MARY USED THE LANGUAGE SHE DID BECAUSE SHE ONLY KNEW A HANDFUL OF ADJECTIVES. ALL OF THEM FOUR LETTERED.
THAT #!%* IS THE MOST $!#@ KIND OF *?#<> IN THE WHOLE %*@!! WORLD!

OTHERS THOUGHT IT WAS BECAUSE SHE MERELY COPIED THE FOULNESS OF THE MUSIC AND MOVIES SHE ABSORBED.
#!@!*
%*$¢
#*!$

STILL OTHERS SAID IT WAS BECAUSE THAT'S HOW HER PARENTS SPOKE...
WHAT A #!?$# CUTE *!%¢* BABY GIRL!
!*%$ RIGHT DEAR!
#!@

...OR PERHAPS SHE WAS JUST REPEATING THE PHRASES OF HER FRIENDS.
#!$*
#!$*
#!$*
#!$*

BUT MARY KNEW THAT HER FOUL MOUTH WAS REALLY A REFLECTION OF A PROBLEM INSIDE OF HER — A FOUL HEART.
#!?$@

ONE DAY MARY HEARD SOMEONE REPEAT SOMETHING JESUS SAID...
"THE GOOD MAN BRINGS GOOD THINGS OUT OF THE GOOD STORED UP IN HIS HEART, AND THE EVIL MAN BRINGS EVIL THINGS OUT OF THE EVIL STORED UP IN HIS HEART. FOR OUT OF THE OVERFLOW OF HIS HEART HIS MOUTH SPEAKS." (LUKE 6:45).

FOUL MOUTH MARY GOT DOWN ON HER KNEES AND ASKED GOD TO CLEAN UP HER DIRTY HEART. AND HE DID!
JESUS, PLEASE FIX MY #!*?#@ LIFE!

THEN A FUNNY THING HAPPENED. THE FOULNESS STARTED TO FADE AWAY. AND OTHERS NOTICED!
THAT IS A VERY DELIGHTFUL BOOK.
MARY??

AND FROM THEN ON "FOUL MOUTH MARY" BECAME KNOWN AS "SWEET MOUTH MARY."

10

3

ONE DAY MARY HEARD SOMEONE REPEAT SOMETHING JESUS SAID...

"THE GOOD MAN BRINGS GOOD THINGS OUT OF THE GOOD STORED UP IN HIS HEART, AND THE EVIL MAN BRINGS EVIL THINGS OUT OF THE EVIL STORED UP IN HIS HEART. FOR OUT OF THE OVERFLOW OF HIS HEART HIS MOUTH SPEAKS" (LUKE 6:45).

8

5

ONCE UPON A TIME THERE WAS A YOUNG LADY WHOSE LANGUAGE COULD PEEL THE PAINT FROM A FENCE. HER NAME WAS "FOUL MOUTH MARY."
* !! $ % $ @ # ? < >

2

AND FROM THEN ON "FOUL MOUTH MARY" BECAME KNOWN AS "SWEET MOUTH MARY."

11

OTHERS THOUGHT IT WAS BECAUSE SHE MERELY COPIED THE FOULNESS OF THE MUSIC AND MOVIES SHE ABSORBED.
#!@!*
%*$¢
#*!#

4

FOUL MOUTH MARY GOT DOWN ON HER KNEES AND ASKED GOD TO CLEAN UP HER DIRTY HEART. AND HE DID!
JESUS, PLEASE FIX MY #!*?$@ LIFE!

9

...OR PERHAPS SHE WAS JUST REPEATING THE PHRASES OF HER FRIENDS.
#!$*
#!$*
#!$*
#!$*

6

BUT MARY KNEW THAT HER FOUL MOUTH WAS REALLY A REFLECTION OF A PROBLEM INSIDE OF HER — A FOUL HEART.
#!?$@

7

The Trap Door

Focus of the Lesson: God does not want anyone to end up in hell. It is our rejection of His gift of Jesus Christ that sends us to hell.
Biblical Basis: Matthew 13:40-42; 18:8,9; Mark 9:43; Luke 16:23-26; 2 Peter 3:9; Revelation 14:10,11; 20:15
Materials Needed: Three copies of "The Trap Door" booklet for each student, card stock, magazines, scissors, felt-tip pens, glue, paper.

Step 1—Approach to the Word
Tell your students: **Imagine that you are on a jury where you must make a decision on the following case. A young man decided to take a shortcut into town across a railroad trestle. There was a warning sign clearly posted and "no trespassing" signs all along the trestle but they were ignored by the young man. When the guy was halfway across the trestle, a train came around the corner. Seeing that there was nowhere on the trestle to go for safety, he decided to jump over the edge and risk a 30-foot drop to the riverbed below. As a result of the fall, the young man suffered broken bones and other injuries. He is now asking you, the jury, to find the railroad company responsible to pay for his injuries and other emotional damages since they created the trestle knowing that it could be conceived of by some as a shortcut into town. Do you find in favor of the young man or of the railroad company?**

Take a vote and see who wins the lawsuit. Transition to the lesson by saying, **Many of you found it incredible that a person would blame someone else for his or her own choices. Today we are going to take a look at the choices a person makes that determine his or her eternal destiny.**

Step 2—Bible Exploration
Divide your class into groups of four to six students. Make sure each student has a Bible. Distribute card stock, glue, magazines, scissors and felt-tip pens to each group and ask them to read the following passages: Matthew 13:40-42; 18:8,9; Mark 9:43; Luke 16:23-26; Revelation 14:10,11; 20:15. (Write them on the chalkboard or an overhead.) Ask each group to create a large postcard from hell, based on what they have read about it in Scripture, using images from the magazines and any that they need to create or modify with their felt-tip pens. Give your groups a time limit. Share and display postcards.

Point out that the images of hell described in the Bible depict a situation that no one will enjoy. Read 2 Peter 3:9 to your students and point out that God has no desire to see people end up in hell.

Step 3—Life Exploration
Pass out copies of "The Trap Door" booklet to your class. Note that many people complain that a loving God would never send anyone to hell. Ask your class to read the booklet and then be prepared to answer the following questions: (Write them on the chalkboard or overhead.)
1. Do you think heaven or hell is gained by the goodness or badness of our behaviors? Why or why not?
2. Do you think people who choose to live without God in this life realize that they have made eternal decisions? If not, do you think they would live differently if they knew that they would have to live forever without God?
3. Do you think God sends people to hell, or that people choose hell when they choose not to serve Christ?
4. How would you explain hell to a person who says a loving God would never send anyone there?

Step 4—Conclusion
Ask your students to think of persons they know who might be helped by "The Trap Door" booklet. Hand out extra copies and ask your students to bow in prayer asking God to give them an opportunity to pass along the booklets to friends.

HOW TO KEEP FROM SENDING YOURSELF TO HELL.

It is always God's desire that people spend eternity with Him. But quite often people choose to resist His love and will in their lives. This resistance of God and his commands is what is called sin and all human beings have sinned plenty of times. The good news is that you can be forgiven for all that rebellion and wrongdoing. Jesus Christ, the perfect God/man died on the cross so that if you put your trust in Him, you can be forgiven and live as part of His family forever.

HOW TO KEEP FROM SENDING YOURSELF TO HELL.

It is always God's desire that people spend eternity with Him. But quite often people choose to resist His love and will in their lives. This resistance of God and his commands is what is called sin and all human beings have sinned plenty of times. The good news is that you can be forgiven for all that rebellion and wrongdoing. Jesus Christ, the perfect God/man died on the cross so that if you put your trust in Him, you can be forgiven and live as part of His family forever.

HEY!! WHERE AM I? WHAT'S GOING ON? THE LAST THING I REMEMBER WAS THAT BIG MAC TRUCK COMING HEAD ON...

(GOD DOES NOT WANT) ANYONE TO PERISH, BUT EVERYONE TO COME TO REPENTANCE
(2 PETER 3:9).

I SUPPOSE THIS WILL DROP ME STRAIGHT INTO H - E - DOUBLE HOCKEY STICKS!

WELL, I'M NOT GOING TO GIVE HIM THE PRIVILEGE OF HUMILIATING ME! HE TRIED TO PUSH HIS WAY ON ME WHILE I WAS ON EARTH. I WOULDN'T ACCEPT HIS WILL THEN AND I WON'T NOW! BESIDES... I DON'T SEE ANY OF MY FRIENDS AROUND THIS PLACE!
CRANK!

WELL IT SEEMS LIKE A RAW DEAL TO ME! AFTER ALL, I WAS A PRETTY NICE GUY ON EARTH. I RECYCLED CANS, TOOK IN STRAY CATS. I SURE WASN'T SOME KINDA HITLER OR ANYTHING!

JUST BECAUSE I DIDN'T BOW AND SCRAPE ALL RELIGIOUSLY ON EARTH IS NO REASON TO YANK DOWN THE LEVER!

The Weird Little Geek

Focus of the Lesson: Christians are called to care for those whom others ignore or despise.
Biblical Basis: Luke 5:12-15
Materials Needed: Copies of "The Weird Little Geek" booklet, paper, pencils.

Step 1—Approach to the Word

Before class write the following situations on separate pieces of paper and hang them in different locations in the room: "Suicide," "Live as a Hermit," "Move Away to Where I Am Unknown" and "Make the Best of It." Tell your students to imagine themselves in the following predicament. They have been involved in a horrible car accident in which they were burned terribly. After much hospital time and many surgeries, they cannot eat, see or speak. Their appearances are a frightful twisted mass of scars. Ask them to look around the room and go to the sign that would best represent how they think they would respond to this situation.

Transition to the lesson by pointing out that terrible accidents do happen to people. For those of us who are blessed to be "normal," it is often hard to imagine ourselves being placed in a position where we are repulsive, a misfit or one of the unlovely. Tell your students, **Today we will be looking at how Jesus handled those whom all the rest of His culture avoided.**

Step 2—Bible Exploration

Have each of your students read Luke 5:12-15. Briefly explain that the disease of leprosy was greatly feared by people and largely untreatable until recently. Lepers had to live away from the rest of the community and warn people if they were in the vicinity. A leper could not have contact with any loved ones for fear of spreading the disease.

Ask your students to write a page in the journal of the leper who was in the Bible story on that fateful day. Tell your students to assume that the leper was not expecting to run into Jesus when his day began and that he would have most likely gone about the business of begging for charity if he hadn't seen Him.

Ask students to read their journal entries. Note especially those journals that capture the sense of the leper's loneliness and despair before meeting Jesus.

Step 3—Life Exploration

Point out to your students that we still have people who are treated as "lepers" in our society—even in our schools. These people have no disease. They are the geeks, the awkward, the weird or the ugly teens whom everyone avoids.

Break into groups of students. Ask your students to reenact how a teen like this might be treated at lunch time, especially if he or she wanted to sit with the students at the "popular" table.

Have students perform skits for the whole group. Then have the students do the skits again, but this time ask for there to be a few students at the popular table who are Christians and who have determined to treat others with the same kind of healing love that Christ demonstrated.

Pass out a copy of "The Weird Little Geek" booklet to each student. Discuss with your class whether it could be possible that students are frozen out of your Christian youth group because they are a little odd.

Step 4—Conclusion

Ask each person in the room to think of one person he or she knows of who is treated like a leper. In a time of silent prayer, invite them to tell God what they will do this week to show those people the love of Christ in a tangible way.

How we treat people does matter. As Christians, we are not entitled to have any kind of smug or superior attitude. How we treat people says volumes about the conditions of our own hearts. Every person counts, especially to God. In fact, God himself identifies with those who are the underdogs of society.

Jesus said, "Whatever you did for one of the least of these brothers of mine, you did for me." (Matthew 25:40)

HOW WE TREAT PEOPLE DOES MATTER.
AS CHRISTIANS, WE ARE NOT ENTITLED
TO HAVE ANY KIND OF SMUG OR
SUPERIOR ATTITUDE. HOW WE TREAT
PEOPLE SAYS VOLUMES ABOUT THE
CONDITIONS OF OUR OWN HEARTS.
EVERY PERSON COUNTS, ESPECIALLY
TO GOD. IN FACT, GOD HIMSELF
IDENTIFIES WITH THOSE WHO
ARE THE UNDERDOGS OF SOCIETY.

JESUS SAID, "WHATEVER YOU DID FOR
ONE OF THE LEAST OF THESE BROTHERS
OF MINE, YOU DID FOR ME" (MATTHEW 25:40).

YUCK! WHO IS THAT KID? WHAT A WEIRDO!!!
I DUNNO. I'VE SEEM HIM AROUND SCHOOL.
2

SO, ANGEL #468, PLEASE REPORT ON THE YOUTH GROUP OF 1ST CHURCH.
WELL SIR, I VISITED THERE FOR A FEW WEEKS. AND I'M AFRAID THAT YOU WILL BE VERY DISAPPOINTED WITH THE RESULTS.
11

OH, HORRORS! HE'S COMING THIS WAY! LET'S JUST IGNORE HIM.
HI THERE
4

AS WELL AS AT SCHOOL
ISN'T THAT THE KID THAT HAS BEEN SHOWING UP AT OUR CHURCH?
YEAH! PRETEND YOU DON'T SEE HIM!
9

6

LATER AT YOUTH GROUP
7

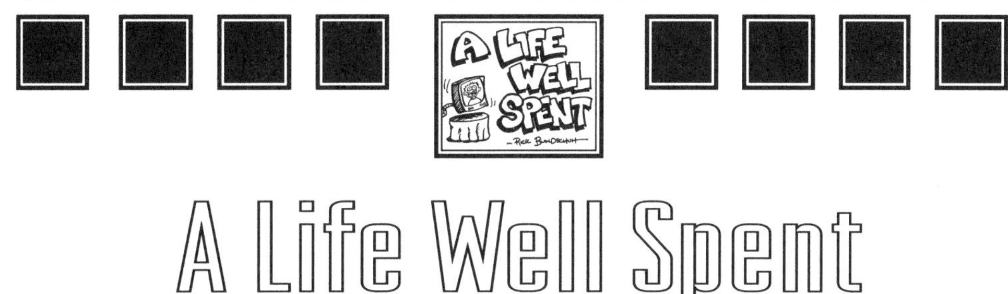

A Life Well Spent

Focus of the Lesson: We must make the most of the time God gives us.
Biblical Basis: Proverbs 28:19; Colossians 4:5; 2 Thessalonians 3:11,12
Materials Needed: Copies of "A Life Well Spent" booklet, chalkboard and chalk, pencils, paper.

Step 1—Approach to the Word

On a chalkboard, write: "What is the greatest waste of time in your life?" As your students come into your class, ask them to write down their ideas on the chalkboard and sign their names to what they have written. (Don't be surprised if a lot of students write down "school.") Discuss the various things written. Talk about things that feel like they are a waste of time but in the long run are not, and things that seem interesting at the moment but in the end are a waste of time.

Step 2—Bible Exploration

Distribute a copy of "A Life Well Spent" booklet, a pencil and paper to everyone in your group. On the chalkboard or overhead write the following passages: Proverbs 28:19; Colossians 4:5; 2 Thessalonians 3:11,12.

Ask your students to read the booklet, look up the passages of Scripture and then create comics of their own showing a person living out the advice from the Word. Have students share their comics. Discuss the idea of misusing time presented in "A Life Well Spent" booklet, particularly in contrast with what we could be investing our time in.

Step 3—Life Exploration

Acknowledge to your class that human beings have a need for rest, relaxation and entertainment. Ask for your students' help in creating the ideal schedule for a Christian teen their age.

Brainstorm the various elements that are found, or should be found, in their daily lives (eating, chores, homework, rest, devotional reading, prayer, hanging out with friends, etc.). Write all the suggestions on the chalkboard or overhead.

Pass out paper and ask your students to each create a pie chart that shows how much time in a typical day they think should be allotted to those activities.

Share pie charts and discuss.

Step 4—Conclusion

Ask your students to consider one area of their lives where they are not using their time as a wise investment. Ask those who are willing to share their areas. On slips of paper, have your students write down their unproductive times and how they would better invest their time this week. Ask them to fold the papers up and take them home as reminders of what they ought to do in those areas of their lives. Close in prayer.

IT HAS BEEN SAID THAT GOD GIVES EACH HUMAN BEING AN HOURGLASS, A BAG OF TOOLS AND AN INSTRUCTION MANUAL. HE EXPECTS US TO MAKE SOMETHING OF OURSELVES WITH THE TIME AND SKILL WE HAVE. HE GIVES US GUIDANCE FROM THE BIBLE, HIS WORD. PERHAPS ONE OF THE GREATEST SINS WE CAN COMMIT IS TO WASTE OUR LIVES AWAY!

"BE CAREFUL, THEN, HOW YOU LIVE NOT AS UNWISE BUT AS WISE, MAKING THE MOST OF EVERY OPPORTUNITY, BECAUSE THE DAYS ARE EVIL" (EPHESIANS 5:15,16).

IT HAS BEEN SAID THAT GOD GIVES EACH HUMAN BEING AN HOURGLASS, A BAG OF TOOLS AND AN INSTRUCTION MANUAL. HE EXPECTS US TO MAKE SOMETHING OF OURSELVES WITH THE TIME AND SKILL WE HAVE. HE GIVES US GUIDANCE FROM THE BIBLE, HIS WORD. PERHAPS ONE OF THE GREATEST SINS WE CAN COMMIT IS TO WASTE OUR LIVES AWAY!
"BE CAREFUL, THEN, HOW YOU LIVE NOT AS UNWISE BUT AS WISE, MAKING THE MOST OF EVERY OPPORTUNITY, BECAUSE THE DAYS ARE EVIL" (EPHESIANS 5:15,16).
A LIFE WELL SPENT
~ RICK BUNDSCHUH

HEY, GEORGE. THIS IS JUNIOR, WANNA GO DO SOMETHING?

BUSY? BUSY DOING WHAT? ALL YOU DO IS SIT IN FRONT OF THAT TV ALL DAY LONG!
I'M LEARNING STUFF, MA.
AND WE'RE HERE ON GILLIGAN'S ISLAND ♪

JUNIOR... ARE YOU LISTENING TO ME?
MOM! OUT OF THE WAY! I'M MISSING A GOOD COMMERCIAL.

JUNIOR, DO YOU KNOW HOW LONG IT HAS BEEN SINCE WE HAVE HAD A GOOD TALK? I MEAN A TALK WITHOUT THE TV BLARING! ONE WHERE I HAVE YOUR UNDIVIDED ATTENTION.
HUH?

JUNIOR ... OH, JUNIOR ... JUNIOR ??
WHAT DAYA WANT, MA? I'M BUSY!
CLICK!

2

I DUNNO. I THOUGHT WE'D RENT A VIDEO OR SOMETHING.

11

WELL, YOU WOULD NEVER KNOW IT BY YOUR GRADES.
HUH? WHUT DID YA SAY?
AND NOW BACK TO OUR SHOW!

4

THAT'S IT!! THE TV IS OFF RIGHT NOW! STOP WASTING YOUR LIFE. GO AND FIND SOMETHING ELSE TO DO!

9

THE KIND OF TRASH THAT THEY PUT ON NOWADAYS IS TERRIBLE.
GAY MIDGET AXE MURDERERS- NEXT ON DONAHUE.
AW, IT AIN'T SO BAD.

6

BESIDES, IT'S SUCH A NICE DAY OUTSIDE, A YOUNG MAN LIKE YOU SHOULD BE OUT GETTING EXERCISE!
I'M EXERCISING MY REMOTE THUMB.

7

The Acorn

Focus of the Lesson: We must die to ourselves to become the kind of people that God can make us.
Biblical Basis: John 12:24-26
Materials Needed: Copies of "The Acorn" booklet, felt-tip pens, butcher paper, tape.

Step 1—Approach to the Word

Divide your room into two sections: "Agree" and "Disagree." Read the following statements and ask your students to move to one side of the room or the other depending on whether they agree or disagree with what is being said:

Everyone has an equal chance at success.

You can do anything you want to if you really put your mind to it.

If God rules a person's life, nothing bad will ever happen to him or her.

I live up to the potential I have.

God is more concerned about making people holy than happy.

Tell your students, **Today we will take a look at the secret of living a life that makes a difference, maximizes our potential and gives us meaning and purpose.**

Step 2—Bible Exploration

Distribute a copy of "The Acorn" booklet to each person in your group. Ask your students to read the story and the passage from the Bible at the end of the booklet—John 12:24-26.

Discuss the symbolism in the booklet and Scripture and what it means. Ask, **What does the seed represent? What does the tree represent? What does it mean for us to "die to ourselves"? How do we do that? Why does it seem scary or hard to do that?**

Step 3—Life Exploration

Ask your class to form groups of four to six students. Give each group a large sheet of butcher paper and a pile of felt-tip pens. Ask each group to create a mural illustrating Christian teens in the act of dying to themselves.

After 15 minutes or so, ask your students to share with the whole group what they have drawn.

Step 4—Conclusion

Invite students to go to any mural they choose and write their names beside some act of dying to self that they will attempt to practice this week. Close in prayer.

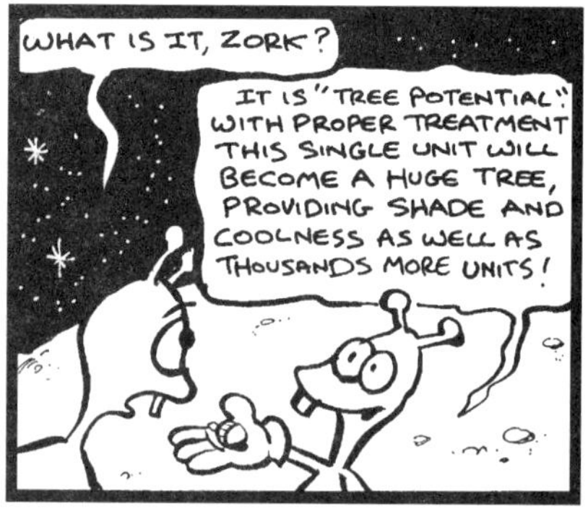

JESUS SAID, "UNLESS A KERNAL OF WHEAT FALLS TO THE GROUND AND DIES, IT REMAINS ONLY A SINGLE SEED. BUT IF IT DIES, IT PRODUCES MANY SEEDS. THE MAN WHO LOVES HIS LIFE WILL LOSE IT, WHILE THE MAN WHO HATES HIS LIFE IN THIS WORLD WILL KEEP IT FOR ETERNAL LIFE" (JOHN 12:24, 25).

Jesus said, "Unless a kernal of wheat falls to the ground and dies, it remains only a single seed. But if it dies, it produces many seeds. The man who loves his life will lose it, while the man who hates his life in this world will keep it for eternal life" (John 12:24, 25).

THE ACORN
Rick Bundschuh—
-ZORK-

10

3

BUT HOW DOES THIS WONDERFUL DISCOVERY WORK, O, ZORK?

SIMPLE! MERELY PUT THIS TREE POTENTIAL IN THE GROUND AND POUR VAST AMOUNTS OF WATER UPON IT.

8

5

SOMEWHERE IN THE GALAXY...
SAUCER 701 LANDING FROM MISSION TO THE PLANET EARTH !!
ZORK IS HOME !

WE WILL PUT IT IN A NICE SAFE PLACE AND WAIT FOR THE TREE POTENTIAL TO ERUPT INTO A COOL GREEN TREE !!
AND THEY ARE STILL WAITING !

2

11

THE GREEN ITEMS WE HAVE OBSERVED ARE CALLED "TREES"... AND THEY ARE MUCH TOO LARGE TO BRING BACK HOME IN OUR VEHICLES.

WHAT ?? YOU MEAN KILL IT ?
WELL... I SUPPOSE SO...
DROWN & BURY ?
WELL, I GUESS...

4

9

WHAT IS IT, ZORK ?
IT IS "TREE POTENTIAL" WITH PROPER TREATMENT THIS SINGLE UNIT WILL BECOME A HUGE TREE, PROVIDING SHADE AND COOLNESS AS WELL AS THOUSANDS MORE UNITS !

WE WILL SOON BE ABLE TO MAKE OUR BARREN PLANET AS GREEN AND COOL AS EARTH !
WONDERFUL
A MARVELOUS GIFT !

6

7

The Disgruntled Shepherd

Focus of the Lesson: God can bless those who feel they are nobodies.
Biblical Basis: Deuteronomy 10:18; Matthew 4:18-22; 8:1-4; 9:9-12; 16:1-4; 19:16-22; Luke 2:8-15; 16:19-31; James 2:5
Materials Needed: Copies of "The Disgruntled Shepherd" booklet, poster board, felt-tip pens, 3x5-inch cards, pencils.
Before Class: Write down a list of the Scriptures found in the Biblical Basis section in a format that is large enough for all of the students to see. An overhead, poster or chalkboard would all work well.

Note: While this lesson can be used anytime of the year, timing it with the Christmas season may give it more impact.

Step 1—Approach to the Word

On a chalkboard or overhead write the following statement: "My life would be much happier if...." Pass out index cards and pencils. Ask students to think seriously about how they might answer this question. Have students write their responses on the cards and then post the cards on a wall. Discuss the various things that students might have listed (lots of money, talent, different parents, more brains, better looks, etc.).

Transition to the lesson by saying, **Many times we look at the lives of others and say to ourselves, "If I had what they have, I would be happy." We often see ourselves as disadvantaged and nobodies. If you have ever felt that way, then what we are going to study today can give you a lot of hope!**

Step 2—Bible Exploration

Divide your class into groups of four to six students. Give each group a large sheet of poster board and felt-tip pens. Tell them that they are to divide the board into three columns. One column will be headed "Loser," one will be labeled "Winner" and the last column should be labeled "Blessed by God."

Hang up the list of passages that you have prepared beforehand for your students to read.

Ask each group to:
1. **Look up and read each passage.**
2. **Decide if the person talked about in the passage would have been judged by his or her society as a winner or loser. Write his or her name or description in the appropriate column.**
3. **Make a mark in the last column if this person was blessed or seemed to be used by God.**

Your students should discover that most of the people in the Bible that were blessed or used by God were not from the category that the society of their times would have described as being winners!

Step 3—Life Exploration

Distribute copies of "The Disgruntled Shepherd" booklet to your class. Ask your group to read through the booklets. Then talk about the disappointments that the character in the story felt and what God did for him. Discuss whether his situation was because he made bad choices, or hard yet necessary choices.

Discuss the kind of disappointments that are common for students who are the age of your group. Ask, **In what ways might God step in to give hope or joy to someone who finds his or her dream dashed through no real fault of his or her own?**

Step 4—Conclusion

Pass out card stock and felt-tip pens to your students. Ask students to create Christmas cards that God might send to them as a source of hope that He will use them if they trust Him with their lives. Share cards and close in prayer.

How to Find Hope This Christmas

Almost two thousand years ago God stepped onto this earth disguised as a human being. He was born in a stable to poor peasant folk. He lived in obscurity most of His life. He never wrote a book, marshaled an army, ran for political office or won a medal, yet He has brought more hope, joy and inspiration to humankind than anyone else in history. To discover His love for yourself, simply invite Him to be the Lord of your life and to cleanse you from your sins. It could be the best Christmas of your life.

 © 1995 by Gospel Light. Permission to photocopy granted.

RATS! I'VE PULLED THE GRAVEYARD SHIFT AGAIN!
SCHEDULE
ACME SHEEP CARE INC.

2

"THE LORD IS GOOD TO THOSE WHOSE HOPE IS IN HIM"
(LAMENTATIONS 3:25).
I JUST SAW A BABY KING!
WELL, DO YOU STILL THINK YOU'RE FORSAKEN?

11

STUCK ON GRAVEYARD AGAIN, ABE? I HOPE YA BROUGHT YOUR LONG UNDERWEAR. IT'S GONNA BE A COLD ONE... HA! HA! HA!
SHUT UP, ZEKE!!

4

GACK!! WHAT'S THAT?

9

I COULD HAVE GONE TO SCHOOL, GOTTEN AN EDUCATION AND A GREAT JOB! INSTEAD I'M STRUGGLING TO MAKE A BUCK AS A LOUSY SHEPHERD!!
SORRY, BUT SOMEBODY HAS TO WATCH ME.

6

LOOK AT THE LIGHTS BLAZING FROM THE PALACE. OBVIOUSLY A HUGE PARTY WITH THE KING! WHAT I WOULDN'T GIVE TO MEET THE KING. FAT CHANCE FOR A CRUMMY SHEPHERD.

7

The Temptation

Focus of the Lesson: Temptation is often the right thing under the wrong conditions.
Biblical Basis: Joshua 6:1,2,17-19; 7:1-26
Materials Needed: Copies of "The Temptation" booklet, large sheets of butcher paper, felt-tip pens, pencils, paper, rat trap, a 5- or 10-dollar bill, chopsticks.

Step 1—Approach to the Word
Locate a rat trap (a rat trap is an extra large and intimidating mouse trap, but a mouse trap will do if you cannot find one of these granddaddy models) and a number of cheap chopsticks. Wedge money into the trap and set it. As your students come into the room hand them a pair of chopsticks. Tell students that they can keep the money in the trap if they can get it out using the chopsticks *without snapping* the trap. Your money will probably be safe unless you have some future engineers in your group.

Transition to the lesson by saying, **For some of you, this little amount of money was not enough to get you interested in messing with the snapping mechanism of the trap. For others, it was sufficient bait. Today we are going to consider the nature of temptation and the trap that it often becomes.**

Step 2—Bible Exploration
Have your class get into groups of four to six students. Pass out a large sheet of butcher paper (for a mural) and felt-tip pens to each group.

Ask each group to read Joshua 6:1,2,17-19; 7:1-26 and then create a mural that depicts the events in the passages. (Option: Have your students work individually to create a daily journal showing the possible thoughts of Achan.)

Post the murals and discuss the problem of Achan's sin. Point out that it was not normally wrong for soldiers to take booty for themselves from cities they captured. Note that the problem with Achan's actions was that he took his goodies after he had been told they were off-limits. The goods themselves were not evil, but rather the actions that surrounded them were.

Step 3—Life Exploration
Distribute a copy of "The Temptation" booklet to each person in the class. Ask students to read the comics and then give examples from the life of a teenager of how something good could be contained or surrounded by a wrong condition. Write down their ideas on a chalkboard or overhead. Now ask your group to come up with a list of criteria to help a person see when a condition is wrong or right. Again, write the ideas of the group on the chalkboard or overhead.

Step 4—Conclusion
Pass out blank paper and pencils to your students and ask them to draw pictures of something that is "bait" for them. Close in prayer by asking God for the wisdom to recognize temptation.

THE PROBLEM WITH MOST TEMPTATIONS IS NOT THE "BAIT" BUT RATHER THE CONDITIONS THAT SURROUND IT. GOD HAS CREATED SOME WONDERFUL AND EXCITING THINGS FOR PEOPLE TO ENJOY AND USE. MONEY, SEX, FRIENDS AND A JOB CAN ALL TURN INTO TROUBLE IF THE SITUATIONS AROUND THEM ARE WRONG. GOD WANTS TO LEAD US OUT OF TEMPTING SITUATIONS BUT IT IS OFTEN UP TO US TO BE WISE ENOUGH TO KNOW WHEN A GOOD THING IS SURROUNDED BY THE WRONG CIRCUMSTANCES.

THE PROBLEM WITH MOST TEMPTATIONS IS NOT THE "BAIT" BUT RATHER THE CONDITIONS THAT SURROUND IT. GOD HAS CREATED SOME WONDERFUL AND EXCITING THINGS FOR PEOPLE TO ENJOY AND USE. MONEY, SEX, FRIENDS AND A JOB CAN ALL TURN INTO TROUBLE IF THE SITUATIONS AROUND THEM ARE WRONG. GOD WANTS TO LEAD US OUT OF TEMPTING SITUATIONS BUT IT IS OFTEN UP TO US TO BE WISE ENOUGH TO KNOW WHEN A GOOD THING IS SURROUNDED BY THE WRONG CIRCUMSTANCES.

WAKE UP, EARL, IT'S THE ANSWER TO OUR DREAMS AND PRAYERS!
HUH?

WHACK

NO MORE TROUBLES!

WHAT'S THE MATTER WITH YOU, EARL? IT'S JUST A BIT OF WOOD, WIRE AND METAL. STUFF WE SEE AROUND THIS PLACE ALL OF THE TIME!!

WHOA! JUNIOR, HOLD ON! NOT SO FAST!
FOOD! FOOD FOOD! FOOD!

SOMETHING'S NOT RIGHT HERE!
WHAT'S THE PROBLEM? WE'RE TALKIN' FOOD HERE!

A Case of the Guilties!!

Focus of the Lesson: God wants to deliver us from the terrible feeling of guilt.
Biblical Basis: Matthew 26:31-35,69-75; 27:1-10; Luke 22:1-6,47,48; Acts 16:22-34
Materials Needed: Copies of "A Case of the Guilties" booklet, paper, pencils.

Step 1—Approach to the Word
Distribute a copy of "A Case of the Guilties" booklet to each student. Ask students to read the booklets and then ask your group to comment on Belinda's behavior. **Does this kind of thing happen to people? Should Belinda have been guilty? Was her attempt to avoid people really a solution to the guilt she was feeling? Why or why not? What would be the difference between the guilt that Belinda was feeling and false guilt?**

Transition to the lesson by saying, **Everyone has felt guilty at one time or another. Guilt is really a good thing in most cases. It is the feeling of discomfort that we get when we violate what we know to be the right and godly thing to do. Today we are going to look at how people end up with the guilties and how they can get rid of them.**

Step 2—Bible Exploration
Divide your group into three separate groups, or if you have a large class, into multiples of three with no more than six students in any one group.

Assign Group One the following: **Read Acts 16:22-34 and then create a short melodrama showing what the jailer did and probably felt.**

Assign Group Two the following: **Read Matthew 27:1-10; Luke 22:1-6,47,48 and then create a series of live snapshots that show what took place in this passage and the actions and probable feelings of Judas.**

Assign Group Three the following: **Read Matthew 26:31-35,69-75 and then create a TV talk show showing what went on in the passage.** (You know, "Today at noon. Women who are proud to grow a beard.")

Have each group perform for the whole group. Point out the situation that each of the individuals in the passage got himself into and the guilt and shame that he felt.

Let your students know that God has made a way for guilt to be washed away and for the kind of behavior that causes guilt to be brought under control.

Step 3—Life Exploration
Pass out pencils and paper. Ask your students to imagine that guilt is a disease. Tell them that they are part of the Divine Pharmacy Company and that they should write out a prescription that would enable people to be cured of the disease of guilt.

Read and post the results.

Step 4—Conclusion
Ask your students to quietly consider something they have done recently, for which they feel the pain of guilt. Have a time of quiet prayer asking God to forgive them for those deeds and free their hearts of the heaviness of guilt.

Most people feel guilty because they are! Guilt is that nagging feeling that you have done something wrong, stupid, shameful or evil. It is what a person feels when he or she knows what is right but does what is wrong. Like pain that accompanies a wound, guilt is the soul's way of telling us that we are doing spiritual damage. We can try to block guilt out but like an acid it eats through our best defenses and haunts us again.

The good news is that you can be free from guilt. Jesus Christ died on the cross to forgive you of every wrong, stupid, shameful or evil thing you have ever done. By trusting in Him and living a lifestyle that tries to follow in His steps, we can erase the "guilties" forever! And that is very good news!

Most people feel guilty because they are! Guilt is that nagging feeling that you have done something wrong, stupid, shameful or evil. It is what a person feels when he or she knows what is right but does what is wrong. Like pain that accompanies a wound, guilt is the soul's way of telling us that we are doing spiritual damage. We can try to block guilt out but like an acid it eats through our best defenses and haunts us again.

The good news is that you can be free from guilt. Jesus Christ died on the cross to forgive you of every wrong, stupid, shameful or evil thing you have ever done. By trusting in Him and living a lifestyle that tries to follow in His steps, we can erase the "guilties" forever! And that is very good news!

HI, BELINDA, HOW ARE YOU?
UH... WHY, FINE, PASTOR.
OH MY GOODNESS, PASTOR DAVE IS EXTRA FRIENDLY THIS SUNDAY... I WONDER WHAT HE KNOWS.

2

HEY, BELINDA, CHURCH IS ABOUT TO START. YA' COMING?
OH MY, SHE'S LEAVING! I HOPE I DIDN'T OFFEND HER. I SHALL HAVE TO MAKE IT A POINT TO GET TO KNOW ALL I CAN ABOUT HER.
GACK!

11

OH NO! HE JUST LOOKED BACK AT ME AND SMILED... HE MUST KNOW MORE THAN THE INCIDENT AT THE PARTY... COULD HE KNOW ABOUT ME SMOKING THAT JOINT WITH SARAH?

4

THAT'S IT FOR ME. I CAN'T COME BACK TO THIS CHURCH EVER AGAIN. THEY KNOW TOO MUCH ABOUT ME. I'M JUST A FAKE IN THEIR EYES.

9

WHAT? HE'S STOPPING TO TALK WITH MY OLD BOYFRIEND, JON. UH-OH... HE'S TAKING HIM INTO HIS OFFICE. THIS IS WORSE THAN I THOUGHT. HE KNOWS WHAT WE DID!!

6

I FEEL.SO...SO... DIRTY... STUPID AND DIRTY. BUT I REALLY THOUGHT I LOVED JON—FOR A WEEK OR SO. IF PASTOR DAVE KNOWS... THEN EVERYONE MUST KNOW BY NOW!

7

The Tiny Little Trail

Focus of the Lesson: Following Christ means parting from the crowd.
Biblical Basis: Matthew 7:13,14
Materials Needed: Copies of "The Tiny Little Trail" booklet, paper, pencils, blank price tags or paper cut to resemble price tags.

Step 1—Approach to the Word

Remind your students of the old saying "The majority is always right." Ask your students to brainstorm a time or situation when the majority has been wrong. Write a list of what they have to say on the chalkboard. Some examples to get students started are: When most people in Germany thought it would be a good idea to elect Hitler, or when people used to believe that odd neighbors were witches or when most people thought that medical problems would be helped by draining off the blood of the victim.

Transition to the lesson by pointing out that just because the majority thinks or does something, does not make it good, wise or just.

Step 2—Bible Exploration

Distribute a copy of "The Tiny Little Trail" booklet to each student. Ask them to read their booklets and then read Matthew 7:13,14.

Pass out paper and pencils and ask your students to write down the moral of the passage in four words or less. Have students share what they have written.

Step 3—Life Exploration

In groups of four to six members, have your students come up with a list of what might happen to friendships and family relationships if a person was to seriously follow Christ. Allow students to share their lists with others.

Step 4—Conclusion

Ask your students to consider for themselves what the price tag is to follow Christ. Pass out the price tags or paper cut to resemble them and ask your students to write down what it would and does cost them to follow Jesus. Close in prayer for those who are fooled into rejecting Christ by the fallacy of there being safety in numbers.

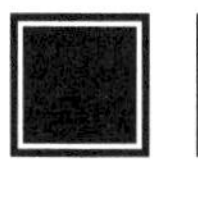

Jesus said, "Enter through the narrow gate. For wide is the gate and broad is the road that leads to destruction, and many enter through it. But small is the gate and narrow the road that leads to life, and only a few find it" (Matthew 7:13, 14).

 © 1995 by Gospel Light. Permission to photocopy granted.

♪ I'M WALKIN' DOWN THE "'OL HIGHWAY OF LIFE." ♪

HEY! DOES ANYONE KNOW WHERE THIS PATH WILL TAKE YOU ??
IT PROBABLY GOES NOWHERE!
LIFE

GOOD! THAT ROAD 'LL LEAD YA NOWHERE FUN!
GEE... IT'S GETTING KINDA FOGGY. MAYBE I SHOULDA TAKEN THAT NARROW LITTLE TRAIL AFTER ALL!

I DON'T KNOW, BUT IT SURE DOESN'T SEEM WELL-TRAVELED. ALL THE COOL PEOPLE ARE ON THIS HIGHWAY.

SIGH... OH WELL!
LIFE

God Beats the Odds

Focus of the Lesson: The magnificence of God is displayed in His creative powers.
Biblical Basis: Nehemiah 9:6; Psalm 104:24; Amos 4:13; Romans 1:20
Materials Needed: Copies of "God Beats the Odds" booklet, dice, a 20-dollar bill, paper, pencils.
Before Class: Be aware of the various ideas about Creation and science in order to prepare for questions that may come up. One good resource that deals with the concepts presented in this lesson is *The Creator and the Cosmos* by Hugh Ross (NavPress, 1993).

Step 1—Approach to the Word
Attach the money to the board with a note saying: **This $20 goes to the first student to roll double sixes four times in a row.** Naturally you must be prepared to part with your money, but as your students start to roll the dice, they will soon see that the odds are not in their favors.

After a few minutes of play, get the class back together and ask, **How long do you think it would take to roll four double sixes in a row? All day? A few hours? A few days? Imagine if I said that you had to roll double sixes a hundred times in a row to win the money. Would any of you have even tried?**

Transition to the lesson by saying, **Today we are going to look at events in which the law of chance works in the favor of those of us who believe that God is the One who created the universe by His Word.**

Step 2—Bible Exploration
Hand each person a sheet of paper. Instruct students to read Nehemiah 9:6; Psalm 104:24; Amos 4:13; Romans 1:20, and then tear the paper into shapes that represent some creation of God that reminds them of God's magnificence. Some may tear the paper into the shape of a heart demonstrating God's love, or a light bulb showing His creativity. Have students share their tear art and explain the significance of their art.

Step 3—Life Exploration
Distribute copies of "God Beats the Odds" booklet to your students. Ask them to comment on their thoughts about the information contained in it.

Ask your students to work individually to create an article for the editorial page of a newspaper that would argue for the idea of a Creator.

Share what has been written.

Step 4—Conclusion
Ask each of your students to write one word that sums up what they have learned about God and His Creation. Invite a few of them to share the significance of the words they have written. Close in prayer.

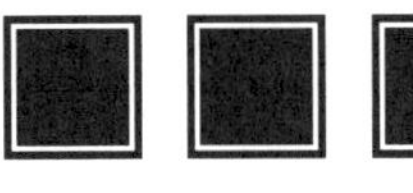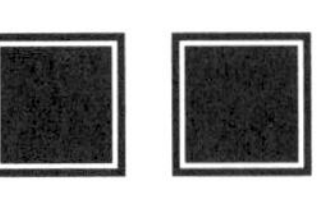

NOW MOST SCIENTISTS BELIEVE THAT THE UNIVERSE IS ONLY AROUND 15 BILLION YEARS OLD. A LONG TIME, BUT NOT NEARLY LONG ENOUGH FOR CHANCE TO, ER, UH, HAVE A CHANCE.

IT OBVIOUSLY TAKES MORE FAITH TO BELIEVE IN CHANCE THAN IT DOES TO BELIEVE THAT THERE IS A CREATOR BEHIND THE EARTH.

THE AMAZING THING IS THAT THE CREATOR OF THE UNIVERSE WANTS US TO KNOW AND LOVE HIM.

HE WANTS IT SO MUCH THAT HE CAME TO EARTH AS A HUMAN AND DIED FOR THE WRONGS OF PEOPLE EVERYWHERE.

YOU CAN KNOW THIS CREATOR YOURSELF! ALL YOU HAVE TO DO IS TO INVITE JESUS CHRIST TO COME INTO YOUR LIFE AND FORGIVE YOU OF ALL YOUR REBELLION AND WRONGDOING. IT WILL BE THE START OF A NEW LIFE AND AN EXCITING NEW ADVENTURE!

YOU CAN KNOW THIS CREATOR YOURSELF! ALL YOU HAVE TO DO IS TO INVITE JESUS CHRIST TO COME INTO YOUR LIFE AND FORGIVE YOU OF ALL YOUR REBELLION AND WRONGDOING. IT WILL BE THE START OF A NEW LIFE AND AN EXCITING NEW ADVENTURE!

IF YOU WANT TO PICTURE WHAT THOSE ODDS ARE REALLY LIKE, IMAGINE THAT YOU COULD TAKE A SHOE BOX AND DUMP A PILE OF DIRT IN IT. THE ODDS THAT YOU COULD SHAKE THE BOX A FEW TIMES AND HAVE THE DIRT ASSEMBLE ITSELF INTO A WATCH TELLING THE CORRECT TIME ARE THE SAME AS LIFE HAPPENING BY CHANCE.

10

NOW MOST SCIENTISTS BELIEVE THAT THE UNIVERSE IS ONLY AROUND 15 BILLION YEARS OLD. A LONG TIME, BUT NOT NEARLY LONG ENOUGH FOR CHANCE TO, ER, UH, HAVE A CHANCE.

3

A LITTLE STRONGER AND LIFE WOULD BE SQUISHED TO A GOOEY PUDDLE.

8

IF THE EARTH WAS A LITTLE CLOSER TO THE SUN, ALL LIFE WOULD BE COOKED TO A CINDER AND THE OCEANS WOULD EVAPORATE.

5

Panel 2

NOT TOO LONG AGO MOST SCIENTISTS ARGUED THAT THE UNIVERSE WAS INFINITELY OLD. THIS MEANT THAT TO GET LIFE AS WE KNOW IT, THE DICE OF CHANCE COULD BE ROLLED AN INFINITE NUMBER OF TIMES, UNTIL ONE DAY THINGS GOT LUCKY!

Panel 11

IT OBVIOUSLY TAKES MORE FAITH TO BELIEVE IN CHANCE THAN IT DOES TO BELIEVE THAT THERE IS A CREATOR BEHIND THE EARTH.

THE AMAZING THING IS THAT THE CREATOR OF THE UNIVERSE WANTS US TO KNOW AND LOVE HIM.

HE WANTS IT SO MUCH THAT HE CAME TO EARTH AS A HUMAN AND DIED FOR THE WRONGS OF PEOPLE EVERYWHERE.

Panel 4

NOT ONLY DO THE ODDS INCREASE DRAMATICALLY WITH A YOUNG UNIVERSE, BUT THEY GET DOWNRIGHT ABSURD WHEN ONE CONSIDERS ALL OF THE FACTORS THAT HAVE TO BE JUST RIGHT FOR LIFE TO TAKE PLACE. FOR EXAMPLE, CONSIDER THE RELATIONSHIP OF THE EARTH TO THE SUN.

Panel 9

THERE ARE DOZENS OF FACTORS LIKE THESE THAT MUST BE JUST RIGHT FOR LIFE AS WE KNOW IT TO EXIST. THE ODDS OF THIS HAPPENING BY CHANCE ARE AT THE BEST 1 IN 10

Panel 6

A LITTLE FARTHER AND EVERYTHING ON EARTH WOULD BE AS FROZEN AS A GIANT POPSICLE.

Panel 7

OR CONSIDER THE EARTH'S GRAVITATIONAL FIELD. JUST A LITTLE WEAKER AND WE WOULD FLOAT OFF INTO SPACE.

The Canyon

Focus of the Lesson: Jesus Christ is our only provision to reach God the Father.
Biblical Basis: John 14:16; Ephesians 2:8,9; 1 Timothy 2:5
Materials Needed: Copies of "The Canyon" booklet, chalkboard and chalk, poster board, felt-tip pens.

Step 1—Approach to the Word

Write on a chalkboard the following incomplete sentence: "The fact that a person is very sincere about what he or she believes...." Ask your students to contribute an ending to the statement. Transition to the lesson by saying, **The fact that someone is sincere is never the criteria or proof that what he or she is sincere about is true. A good way to end this statement would be to say that because someone is sincere does not make him or her right! This is especially true when it comes to spiritual things.**

Step 2—Bible Exploration

Ask your students to form groups of four to six students. Then assign each group one of the following passages: John 14:16; Ephesians 2:8,9; 1 Timothy 2:5. Distribute poster board and felt-tip pens to each group and ask each to create a billboard illustrating the main idea of its assigned verse.

Share posters.

Step 3—Life Exploration

Distribute a copy of "The Canyon" booklet to each student. Ask students to read the comics and locate the various ideas that people think will allow them to override the gap that sin has created between people and God. Discuss any other ideas that people might have as ways to get to God.

Step 4—Conclusion

Ask each student to think of one person to whom he or she could pass on his or her copy of "The Canyon" booklet. Spend some time praying for those individuals and that God would give your students the right opportunities to pass on the booklets.

There is no "magic formula," strange ceremony or special words that must be uttered in order to become a Christian. God looks at the attitude of your heart, which is much more important than the words you say. The following steps are guides to help you see what kind of commitment is needed in order to truly become a Christian:

Step 1- Admit to God that you have done wrong things. Confess that you often make bad decisions and that you are in need of Someone bigger and smarter than you to be the decision maker in your life.

Step 2 - Ask Christ to forgive you for those wrongs and invite Him to be the One who is the decision maker in your life.

Step 3 - Thank Christ for dying for your sins and for making you one of His children forever!

There is no "magic formula," strange ceremony or special words that must be uttered in order to become a Christian. God looks at the attitude of your heart, which is much more important than the words you say. The following steps are guides to help you see what kind of commitment is needed in order to truly become a Christian:

Step 1- Admit to God that you have done wrong things. Confess that you often make bad decisions and that you are in need of Someone bigger and smarter than you to be the decision maker in your life.

Step 2 - Ask Christ to forgive you for those wrongs and invite Him to be the One who is the decision maker in your life.

Step 3 - Thank Christ for dying for your sins and for making you one of His children forever!

10

3

8

5

WOW! IT SURE IS BEAUTIFUL OVER ON THAT SIDE OF THE CANYON.
EVERYONE WANTS TO GET THERE SOMEHOW.
YEAH, BUT HOW DO YA GET FROM THIS DESERT TO PARADISE?

"I AM THE WAY, AND THE TRUTH AND THE LIFE. NO ONE COMES TO THE FATHER EXCEPT THROUGH ME · [JESUS]" (JOHN 14:6).
WELCOME TO HEAVEN
BLOOD OF CHRIST BRIDGE

2

11

OH YUCK! HE DIDN'T MAKE IT!
SPLAT!

WHO ARE THOSE NUTS?
FOLLOW US! WE'VE GOT A SECRET WAY!
EVERY CULT GROUP IMAGINABLE!

4

9

MAKE WAY FOR THE POLE VAULT OF GOOD DEEDS!

CLOSE, BUT NO CIGAR!
NEXT TIME A LONGER POLE

6

7

The Complaint

Focus of the Lesson: God knows and has experienced the hurts and pains that are common to human beings. He knows our suffering.

Biblical Basis: Luke 7:30-34; 22:39-46,54-61,63-65; John 1:10,11; 10:20

Materials Needed: Copies of "The Complaint" booklet, pencils, paper, butcher paper on which you have written "Jesus felt...," felt-tip pens. Optional: a complaint form.

Step 1—Approach to the Word

Ask your students to think of a product that they would like to complain about—something that did not return what it promised or was of inferior quality. Take a few minutes to hear the complaints of your students.

Transition to the lesson by saying, **Now that you've shared your gripes about some of the products you have had experience with, let's take a minute and look at some people who have a gripe against God Himself.**

Step 2—Bible Exploration

Distribute a copy of "The Complaint" booklet to each student. Ask them to read the booklets. Assign each of the following passages to a different student to look up: Luke 7:30-34; 22:39-46,54-61,63-65; John 1:10,11; 10:20.

While your students are reading, hang the large sheet of butcher paper on the wall. Distribute felt-tip pens. Have students write a few words about what Christ endured.

Step 3—Life Exploration

Ask your students to imagine that they are angels at the "Heavenly Complaint Department" with the duty of responding to the gripes of humans. Distribute paper and pencils and ask each student to write down a complaint common to humans. Then write the response that an angel would give referring to the life and suffering of Christ. To make this more fun you may want to create a complaint form on a computer or have the students design one as part of the activity.

Read the various complaints and responses.

Step 4—Conclusion

Give students sheets of paper and ask them to write a prayer of appreciation to God for being willing to live and suffer as a human and for the understanding that He has of what we go through. Close in prayer.

THEN, JUST WHEN YOU NEED THEM MOST, YOU SHOULD BE DESERTED BY ALL OF YOUR FRIENDS AND BETRAYED BY THOSE YOU LOVE AND TRUST!

JESUS CHRIST, ALTHOUGH HE WAS GOD, SET ASIDE THE PRIVILEGES OF BEING DEITY AND BECAME HUMAN. HE SUFFERED AND DIED SO WE COULD HAVE EVERLASTING LIFE AND TO SHOW THAT GOD UNDERSTANDS OUR HURTS AND PROBLEMS. HE ROSE AGAIN FROM THE DEAD SO WE WOULD KNOW THAT HE HAS THE POWER TO ACTUALLY RESCUE US FROM OUR WRONGDOING AND HELP US THROUGH OUR TOUGH SITUATIONS.

THE
COMPLAINT
FINAL JUDGMENT
WAITING AREA
— RICK BUNDSCHUH —

JESUS CHRIST, ALTHOUGH HE WAS GOD, SET ASIDE THE PRIVILEGES OF BEING DEITY AND BECAME HUMAN. HE SUFFERED AND DIED SO WE COULD HAVE EVERLASTING LIFE AND TO SHOW THAT GOD UNDERSTANDS OUR HURTS AND PROBLEMS. HE ROSE AGAIN FROM THE DEAD SO WE WOULD KNOW THAT HE HAS THE POWER TO ACTUALLY RESCUE US FROM OUR WRONG-DOING AND HELP US THROUGH OUR TOUGH SITUATIONS.

WE FEEL THAT YOU AREN'T REALLY IN A POSITION TO JUDGE US — YOU BEING GOD AND ALL.

FINALLY, YOU SHOULD BE TORTURED, BEATEN, HUMILIATED PUBLICALLY AND THEN VERY SLOWLY AND PAINFULLY MURDERED!!

FURTHERMORE, WE THINK YOU SHOULD BE BORN IN POVERTY AND UNDER SUSPICIOUS CIRCUMSTANCES. WE ALSO THINK YOU SHOULD BE BORN TO AN OPPRESSED RACE OF PEOPLE.

EXCUSE ME, LORD, BUT I'VE BEEN ELECTED BY ALL THOSE AWAITING FINAL JUDGMENT TO BRING THIS COMPLAINT.
JUDGMENT AHEAD

NEVER MIND, MY LORD!

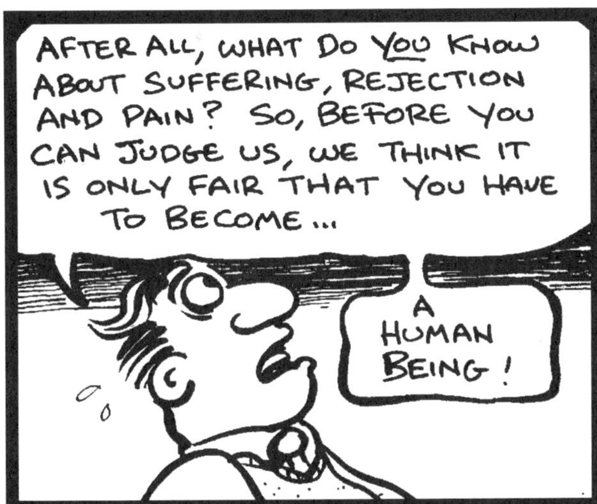

AFTER ALL, WHAT DO YOU KNOW ABOUT SUFFERING, REJECTION AND PAIN? SO, BEFORE YOU CAN JUDGE US, WE THINK IT IS ONLY FAIR THAT YOU HAVE TO BECOME...
A HUMAN BEING!

THEN YOU WILL BE ABLE TO JUDGE US HUMAN BEINGS FAIRLY!!
COMPLAINT

AND WE THINK IT ONLY PROPER THAT YOU BE PERSECUTED AND HATED FOR BEING RIGHT!

THEN, JUST WHEN YOU NEED THEM MOST, YOU SHOULD BE DESERTED BY ALL OF YOUR FRIENDS AND BETRAYED BY THOSE YOU LOVE AND TRUST!

How to Grow as a Christian

Focus of the Lesson: We must grow and mature in our faith.
Biblical Basis: Psalm 105:3; 119:11; Matthew 7:7; Mark 11:25; John 13:34; 1 Thessalonians 5:17; 2 Timothy 2:15,16; Hebrews 4:12,16; 10:24; 1 John 1:9
Materials Needed: Copies of the "How to Grow as a Christian" booklet, large sheets of paper, felt-tip pens, paper, pencils.

Step 1—Approach to the Word

Ask your students to help you come up with a list of the things that are basic ideas or foundations that must be learned and mastered before one can go on in that specific area. For example, in math the basics are addition, subtraction, multiplication and division. Ask your students to help come up with a list of foundations for reading or writing, cooking, driving, swimming, etc.

Transition to the lesson by saying, **In the Christian life there are also basic ideas that must be mastered if we ever hope to grow as Christians. Let's take some time to find out what these are.**

Step 2—Bible Exploration

Divide the students into four groups. Assign one of the following groups of passages to each group to read:
1. Psalm 119:11; 2 Timothy 2:15,16; Hebrews 4:12
2. Psalm 105:3; Matthew 7:7; 1 Thessalonians 5:17; Hebrews 4:16
3. John 13:34; Hebrews 10:24
4. Mark 11:25; 1 John 1:9

Distribute large sheets of paper, felt-tip pens and pencils to each group. After your groups have read the assigned passages, have them create advertisements displaying the basic concept of Christian growth found in their assigned passages that must be mastered and any reasons why this concept is important to know.

Share advertisements.

Step 3—Life Exploration

Pass out paper and pencils to each person. Have students complete each of the following statements on their papers after you have read them. (You may wish to write these incomplete statements on the chalkboard.)

Reading a portion of the Bible every day will...

Prayer helps a person...

Being involved in a good church...

Confessing our wrongdoings to God...

Ask your students to tell how they finished these statements. Note any good insights as your students share what they have written.

Step 4—Conclusion

Pass out paper to each student. Ask them to create report cards and grade themselves on disciplines of the Christian life: devotional reading, prayer, church participation and confessing our wrongdoings. Ask them to give themselves a grade from A to F on each discipline. As you are closing your lesson, distribute copies of the "How to Grow as a Christian" booklet to your students. Encourage them to read the booklet occasionally as a reminder to keep their faith growing.

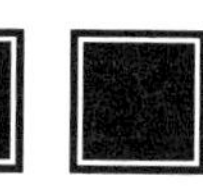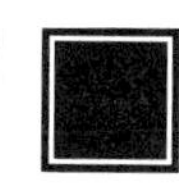

HOW TO GROW
RICK BUNDSCHUH
AS A CHRISTIAN

ALL CHRISTIANS START OUT AS SPIRITUAL BABIES.
THEY NEED TO LEARN HOW TO WALK WITH GOD.

GA GA!
BUT SOME PEOPLE STAY SPIRITUAL BABIES FOR MANY YEARS.
GROWING AS A CHRISTIAN IS IMPORTANT!
THIS BOOKLET CONTAINS TIPS THAT WILL HELP YOU BECOME A WISE, GROWING AND MATURE CHRISTIAN.

THE FIRST THING A PERSON NEEDS TO GROW SPIRITUALLY IS GOOD NOURISHMENT. THE BIBLE IS FOOD FOR A CHRISTIAN.
BIBLE
READ IT EVERY DAY!

THE BIBLE IS ALSO LIKE A MAP TO SHOW YOU WHERE TO GO IN THE JOURNEY OF LIFE. IT IS NOT GOOD ENOUGH JUST TO READ IT, BUT WE MUST FOLLOW ITS DIRECTIONS.
THIS WAY
THAT WAY
WHICH WAY
MAP

SINCE READING THE BIBLE IS VERY IMPORTANT FOR SPIRITUAL GROWTH, YOU WILL WANT TO MAKE SURE TO FIND A TRANSLATION THAT IS EASY TO READ, FOR EXAMPLE, ONE WITHOUT ALL THE "THEES" AND "THOUS".
CREAK!

PRAYER IS ANOTHER IMPORTANT ACTIVITY FOR GROWING AS A CHRISTIAN. PRAYER IS JUST TALKING TO GOD, AND YOU CAN TALK TO HIM ANYWHERE, ANYTIME, ABOUT ANYTHING!
HE LOVES TO HEAR FROM YOU.

IT IS MUCH EASIER TO GROW AS A CHRISTIAN IF YOU SURROUND YOURSELF WITH PEOPLE WHO WANT TO SERVE GOD, TOO. THIS IS ONE REASON IT IS IMPORTANT TO FIND A GOOD ACTIVE CHURCH AND BECOME A PART OF IT.

SOMETIMES YOUNG CHRISTIANS DON'T FEEL PARTICULARLY SPIRITUAL.
SIGH!
SOMETIMES THE ARE SO LOW THAT THEY DOUBT THEY ARE REALLY CHRISTIANS.

FACT
BIBLE
FORTUNATELY, BEING A CHRISTIAN DOESN'T DEPEND ON HOW YOU FEEL, BUT RATHER ON THE FACT THAT YOU ARE A CHILD OF GOD. PUT YOUR FAITH IN THAT FACT — NOT IN FEELINGS!

THE JOURNEY OF A CHRISTIAN IS NOT ALWAYS EASY BUT THE FINAL DESTINATION IS WELL WORTH THE EFFORT.

A Communiqué from Hell

Focus of the Lesson: We need to understand Satan's wiles.
Biblical Basis: John 8:44; 2 Corinthians 11:3,14; Ephesians 6:11-17; 1 Peter 5:8; Revelation 12:9
Materials Needed: Copies of "A Communiqué from Hell" booklet, chalkboard and chalk, large paper, felt-tip pens, a prize, paper, pencils.

Step 1—Approach to the Word
Write the following words without the definitions in the parentheses on the chalkboard:
Subterfuge (Deception)
Ensnare (To catch in a trap)
Dupe (To fool or pull a fast one on)
Perfidious (Faithless, treacherous or disloyal)

Give each student a paper and pencil and ask each of them to write down what he or she thinks the words mean. Give a prize to the one(s) who come closest to the definitions.

Transition to the lesson by saying, **Today we are going to take a look at the way that Satan goes after human beings. We will find that his methods are very similar to the words we have talked about.**

Step 2—Bible Exploration
Divide the class into groups of four to six students. Distribute large sheets of paper and felt-tip pens to each group. Ask them to read the following passages: John 8:44; 2 Corinthians 11:3,14; Ephesians 6:11-17; 1 Peter 5:8; Revelation 12:9. Then have students create warning or caution signs that would alert people as to the activity and wiles of Satan.

Share posters.

Step 3—Life Exploration
Distribute a copy of "A Communiqué from Hell" booklet to each student. Read the booklet aloud. Then ask and discuss the following questions:
Do you believe Satan or evil advertises its presence?
Where do people tend to look for Satan that he is not?
What are some ways that Satan might try to ensnare people?
What are some disguises that evil might dress up in?
What are ways that evil could sneak into a church or youth group?

Step 4—Conclusion
Invite your students to read together Ephesians 6:11-17 as a reminder of what a Christian needs to do to repulse the designs of Satan. Close in prayer.

A COMMUNIQUÉ FROM...
HELL
(OR, THE DEVIL TIPS HIS HAND)
HEY! LOOK AT WHAT I FOUND. SOME KINDA OFFICIAL LETTER. "TO FOULCLATTER, CHIEF OF DEMONIC OPERATIONS, SECTOR 5, MY FETID SIR FOULCLATTER, ALL MISERY TO YOU..."
RICK BUNDSCHUH
WITH APOLOGIES TO C.S. LEWIS

"AS YOU ARE NOW ACTIVE FIELD DIRECTOR IN MY PLACE, I THOUGHT I WOULD REMIND YOU OF OUR SUCCESSFUL METHODS FOR INSURING SIGNIFICANT INROADS AGAINST THE WORK OF OUR ENEMY AND HIS EFFORT TO RESCUE THESE DETESTABLE HUMANS FROM US."
GULP!

"FIRST AND FOREMOST, ALWAYS KEEP UP THE RIDICULOUS IMAGE HUMANS HAVE OF US —THE PESKY MISCHIEF MAKER WHO IS ALL MYTH. MAKE SURE THEY PICTURE US PRANCING AROUND IN RED UNDERWEAR COMPLETE WITH HORNS, TAILS AND TRIDENTS!"

"MAKE THOSE WHO INSIST UPON ACTUALLY BELIEVING IN US THINK THEY SEE US IN THE MOST BENIGN OF IMAGES."
TRICK OR TREAT!!
EEK! THE WORK OF THE DEVIL INFESTING MY NEIGHBORHOOD!

"AND PREVENT THEM FROM SEEING US IN OUR GUISE AS 'ANGELS OF LIGHT.'"
VOTE FOR 'OL SCRATCH
KISS MY BABY TOO!

"IN FACT, MY SHADY FRIEND, DIVERSION IS THE NAME OF THE GAME IF YOU EXPECT TO DINE ON HUMANS. NOTE FOR EXAMPLE, THE EXCELLENT JOB WE HAVE DONE, CAUSING THEM TO LOOK FOR MESSAGES FROM US HIDDEN BACKWARDS ON ROCK ALBUMS."
MRGUMPFROMP EAT YOUR PRUNES RAGLEFRACKEN

"...WHILE THEY NEVER CATCH ON TO THE CONSTANT BARRAGE OF LIES WE FEED THEM THROUGH A MORE SUBTLE MEANS."
CLICK

"KEEP THE TROOPS OF THE ENEMY, THOSE ...GAG, COUGH, SPUTTER...'CHRISTIANS' CONCENTRATING ON THEIR PETTY DIFFERENCES RATHER THAN THE VAST COMMON GROUND THEY SHARE. GET THEM TO USE THEIR WEAPONS AGAINST EACH OTHER AND NOT US!
BIBLE
BIBLE

"DON'T WASTE TIME TRYING TO GET RID OF THE BIBLE STUDIES OR YOUTH GROUPS THAT BELONG TO THE ENEMY. JUST WORK TO ASSURE THEY ARE TEDIOUS, BORING, IRRELEVANT AND CLIQUE-FILLED."
ZZZ
ZZZZ
Z Z Z Z

"PLEASE SINK YOUR FANGS INTO OUR LATEST PLOY, WHICH IS TO MAKE THE FOOLISH HUMANS THINK 'TOLERANCE' IS THE HIGHEST VIRTUE. WITH THIS SCHEME IN PLACE WE CAN GET ANY IDEA OF OURS PAST THEM!"
GAY & LESBIAN HEDGEHOG SOCIETY
AXE MURDERS FOR CONGRESS
PYGMIES FOR EQUAL STATUS
NUDIST FOR CHRIST
LOOTERS AND PROUD

"OUR VULGAR FOE
I'LL DISTRACT HIM, YOU GET THE MEMO... AND DON'T LOSE IT AGAIN OR WE'LL DINE ON YOU!!
WOW! LOOK AT THOSE BABES! THIS SILLY OL' LETTER CAN WAIT!

A COMMUNIQUÉ FROM...
HELL (OR, THE DEVIL TIPS HIS HAND)
HEY! LOOK AT WHAT I FOUND. SOME KINDA OFFICIAL LETTER. "TO FOULCLATTER, CHIEF OF DEMONIC OPERATIONS, SECTOR S, MY FETID SIR FOULCLATTER, ALL MISERY TO YOU..."
RICK BUNDSCHUH
WITH APOLOGIES TO C.S. LEWIS

"PLEASE SINK YOUR FANGS INTO OUR LATEST PLOY, WHICH IS TO MAKE THE FOOLISH HUMANS THINK 'TOLERANCE' IS THE HIGHEST VIRTUE. WITH THIS SCHEME IN PLACE WE CAN GET ANY IDEA OF OURS PAST THEM!"
GAY & LESBIAN HEDGEHOG SOCIETY
NUDIST FOR CHRIST
AXE MURDERS FOR CONGRESS
PYGMIES FOR EQUAL STATUS
LOOTERS AND PROUD!

10

"FIRST AND FOREMOST, ALWAYS KEEP UP THE RIDICULOUS IMAGE HUMANS HAVE OF US —THE PESKY MISCHIEF MAKER WHO IS ALL MYTH. MAKE SURE THEY PICTURE US PRANCING AROUND IN RED UNDERWEAR COMPLETE WITH HORNS, TAILS AND TRIDENTS!"

3

"KEEP THE TROOPS OF THE ENEMY, THOSE ...GAG, COUGH, SPUTTER...'CHRISTIANS' CONCENTRATING ON THEIR PETTY DIFFERENCES RATHER THAN THE VAST COMMON GROUND THEY SHARE. GET THEM TO USE THEIR WEAPONS AGAINST EACH OTHER AND NOT US!"
BIBLE
BIBLE

8

"AND PREVENT THEM FROM SEEING US IN OUR GUISE AS 'ANGELS OF LIGHT.'"
VOTE FOR 'OL SCRATCH
KISS MY BABY TOO!

5

"AS YOU ARE NOW ACTIVE FIELD DIRECTOR IN MY PLACE, I THOUGHT I WOULD REMIND YOU OF OUR SUCCESSFUL METHODS FOR INSURING SIGNIFICANT INROADS AGAINST THE WORK OF OUR ENEMY AND HIS EFFORT TO RESCUE THESE DETESTABLE HUMANS FROM US."

GULP!

2

11

"MAKE THOSE WHO INSIST UPON ACTUALLY BELIEVING IN US THINK THEY SEE US IN THE MOST BENIGN OF IMAGES."

TRICK OR TREAT!!

EEK! THE WORK OF THE DEVIL INFESTING MY NEIGHBORHOOD!

4

9

"IN FACT, MY SHADY FRIEND, DIVERSION IS THE NAME OF THE GAME IF YOU EXPECT TO DINE ON HUMANS. NOTE FOR EXAMPLE, THE EXCELLENT JOB WE HAVE DONE, CAUSING THEM TO LOOK FOR MESSAGES FROM US HIDDEN BACKWARDS ON ROCK ALBUMS."

MRGUMPFROMP EAT YOUR PRUNES RAGLEFRACKEN

6

7

The Binky

Focus of the Lesson: The world does not satisfy our hearts' needs; it only pacifies temporarily. Look to the Lord for satisfaction.
Biblical Basis: Matthew 19:16-22; Philippians 4:12,13
Materials Needed: Copies of "The Binky" booklet, chalkboard and chalk, materials for making a montage—photo magazines, large sheets of paper, scissors, glue.

Step 1—Approach to the Word

Play a game of Hangman on the chalkboard. Write the following sentence on the chalkboard as the mystery to be solved by completing the game: "Many people think the world is a big one of these." The solution is "baby pacifier."

How to play a game of Hangman: Draw 12 short blanks on the board to represent the 12 letters in baby pacifier (with a space to represent the space between the two words). Each student gets at least one chance to guess a letter of the puzzle. If the guess is correct write that letter in the proper blank. If it is not, draw one part of a prisoner being hanged, starting at the noose and working down to hands and feet. If the answer is found before the prisoner is completed, the person who gave the correct answer is the winner.

After the answer is revealed, explain that there seems to be a strange phenomenon occurring in the world: Adults are sucking on baby pacifiers!

Step 2—Bible Exploration

Read Matthew 19:16-22, the story of Jesus and the rich young man. (If any student asks why Jesus seemed to be implying He wasn't good in verse 17, point out that Jesus was asking whether the man believed Him to be good—implying that He was God.)

To be sure everyone understands the story, ask, **What question did the rich young man want Jesus to answer? What did Jesus tell him to do at first? Had the young man done the things Jesus said to do? What did Jesus then tell him to do? Why did the man go away sad?**

Tell your students that the man had a spiritual hunger. He came to Jesus to satisfy that hunger because the thing he tried to satisfy it with—money—simply did not work. Money only temporarily pacified him but it could not permanently satisfy him.

Step 3—Life Exploration

Distribute copies of "The Binky" booklet. Have students read the booklets. Let students suggest things that adults and teens tend to depend on, things that only pacify. Write these on the chalkboard.

Discuss Philippines 4:12,13 and the fact that it is the Lord who provides true and eternal satisfaction for a person's spiritual hunger. Spend some time emphasizing the importance of the truth by telling what God has done in your life, in your family and in your friends' lives. Compare your satisfaction in the Lord with the vaporous nature of the things listed on the chalkboard.

Step 4—Conclusion

Distribute magazines, paper, scissors and glue. Have students work together as a class or in small groups to make one or several photo montages of things that only pacify.

When done, display the results. After a silent prayer of commitment, have students sign their work as a promise to trust only God for real satisfaction.

THE **WORLD** IS LIKE A GIANT PACIFIER!

RICHES, POWER, POPULARITY, PHONY RELIGIONS, HEAVY PARTYING—

ALL THESE AND MANY MORE CAN TEMPORARILY PACIFY OUR NEEDS FOR FULFILLMENT. BUT THEY DON'T TRULY **SATISFY**.

"I KNOW WHAT IT IS TO BE IN NEED, AND I KNOW WHAT IT IS TO HAVE PLENTY. I HAVE LEARNED THE SECRET OF BEING CONTENT IN ANY AND EVERY SITUATION, WHETHER WELL FED OR HUNGRY, WHETHER LIVING IN PLENTY OR IN WANT. I CAN DO EVERYTHING **THROUGH HIM WHO GIVES ME STRENGTH**"

(PHILIPPIANS 4:12, 13).

THE BINKY
TOM FINLEY

IT'S REALLY QUITE SIMPLE, DA DA.
I'M CRYING BECAUSE I'M
HUNGRY! I DON'T WANT
TO BE PACIFIED—I WANT TO BE
SATISFIED!

10

UH-OH! THE BABY'S CRYING.
IT'S HUNGRY AND WANTS
TO BE FED.

3

HE HAS TWO CHOICES:
HE CAN GO TO ALL THE
TROUBLE TO PREPARE
A BOTTLE — CLEAN THE
BOTTLE IN BOILING WATER,
MIX THE FORMULA, HEAT
THE FORMULA, TEST THE
FORMULA, CLEAN UP THE KITCHEN.
... UGH!

5

2

4

9

6

7

THE **WORLD** IS LIKE A GIANT PACIFIER!

RICHES, POWER, POPULARITY, PHONY RELIGIONS, HEAVY PARTYING—

ALL THESE AND MANY MORE CAN TEMPORARILY PACIFY OUR NEEDS FOR FULFILLMENT. BUT THEY DON'T TRULY **SATISFY**.

"I KNOW WHAT IT IS TO BE IN NEED, AND I KNOW WHAT IT IS TO HAVE PLENTY. I HAVE LEARNED THE SECRET OF BEING CONTENT IN ANY AND EVERY SITUATION, WHETHER WELL FED OR HUNGRY, WHETHER LIVING IN PLENTY OR IN WANT. I CAN DO EVERYTHING **THROUGH <u>HIM</u> WHO GIVES ME STRENGTH**"

(PHILIPPIANS 4:12, 13).

11

The Bridge

Focus of the Lesson: Jesus Christ is the bridge from God the Father to us.
Biblical Basis: John 14:6; Acts 4:12; 1 Timothy 2:5
Materials Needed: Copies of "The Bridge" booklet, chalkboard and chalk, puppets or materials to make puppets.
Before Class: Your students are going to plan a Sunday School lesson that they will present to a younger class at a future date. Talk to the leaders of one of the children's classes and set a date for the presentation.

Note: This lesson provides a great opportunity to present the simple gospel claims to your students as well as younger students. If you have unsaved kids in your class, this will be a good time to give them an opportunity to respond to the gospel.

Step 1—Approach to the Word
Have a few volunteers come to the front of the room to compete in a standing broad jump. Measure the results and give the winner a handshake. Say, **That was pretty good. Now let's see someone jump the width of the room on one bound. Anybody?** Point out that, just as it is impossible for even the greatest athlete to jump more than several feet, it is impossible for anyone to bridge the gap between man and God. Anyone, that is, except Jesus.

Step 2—Bible Exploration
Have volunteers come forward. Each is to write one of the Biblical Basis passages on the chalkboard for all to see. Thank the volunteers, then lead a discussion of the meaning and significance of each passage. Point out that the word "mediator" in 1 Timothy 2:5 means "go-between"—someone who bridges the gap between, in this case, God and humanity.

Step 3—Life Exploration
Hand out copies of "The Bridge" booklet. Explain that the booklet is simple and nearly wordless because it is designed for young children who don't read well. **In fact we are going to have some fun designing a Sunday School skit that we will present to little kids later on!**

The rest of this lesson proceeds in three stages: (1) Writing a skit to be performed by hand puppets; (2) making the puppets and any necessary props and scenery; (3) assigning parts and practicing the skit.

First, work with your students to outline a simple plot. Here are some suggestions: Act out the story in the booklet. Jesus meets a little boy who has been trying everything he can think of to find God (including boating, ballooning and so forth). Jesus comes to tell us that He fills the gap between God and people, including the children in the audience.

Once the plot is outlined, let students develop the actual dialogue and action.

Continue with the last two phases—making the puppets and practicing the skit. Incidentally, students who would never play with puppets will happily do so when they realize they are doing it for children.

Step 4—Conclusion
Since your skit will probably be performed some days in the future, get everyone to fill out a sign-up sheet with addresses and phone numbers so you can call or write them as a reminder.

Congratulate everyone on their involvement. Tell your class that you are available to talk to anyone who may desire to come to God through Jesus the bridge.

When ready to make the presentation, make copies of the booklet for the younger kids to enjoy.

THE BRIDGE
?
TOM FINLEY

GRRRRR!

TNT

?

JESUS IS THE BRIDGE.

12 © 1995 by Gospel Light. Permission to photocopy granted.

10

3

8

5

2

11

4

9

6

7

The Carnival of Life

Focus of the Lesson: Christians cannot love both God and the world. They must pay the price of discipleship.
Biblical Basis: Luke 14:25-33; James 4:4,8
Materials Needed: Copies of "The Carnival of Life" booklet, a clear glass of ice water, a clear glass of cola, an empty glass, paper, felt-tip pens, scissors, string, hole punches.

Step 1—Approach to the Word

Show your class the glass of ice water and the glass of cola. Ask your students to describe the good things about a cold glass of water and a cold glass of cola. Have a volunteer come forward to take one of the drinks. Before he or she gets there, fill the third glass mostly full with the water, then add the cola until the mixture is an unappetizing dirty brown. Offer the drink to the volunteer. It will probably be turned down in disgust, but if not, ask, **How much would you be willing to pay for a case of this stuff?**

Tell your class that some things just don't mix. Trying to whistle with a mouth full of crackers and peanut butter is nearly impossible. Mixing oil and water doesn't work. Combining "nitro" and "glycerin" is fool's play. The Bible tells us we cannot mix friendship with the world and friendship with God.

Step 2—Bible Exploration

Have your class form groups of three or four students. Assign each group one of these passages: Luke 14:25-27; Luke 14:28-33; James 4:4. Give each group a sheet of paper, scissors, a hole punch, and a 12-inch piece of string. Say, **There is a price to pay for following Christ. There are things we must give up and turn away from in order to be the kind of people God wants us to be. Make a price tag that features the cost mentioned in your Scripture passages. Write large because we'll hang these on the wall.**

Display the finished price tags and discuss the various costs involved. These costs include family, the world, everything and life itself. Say, **Of course, when Jesus talks about things like hating our family members and our own lives, He doesn't mean that we should all go home and practice hatred. He means that we must always put God first in our hearts, always be willing to pay any price to serve Him and live for Him. Jesus was using powerful imagery to make a powerful point. Being a Christian costs!**

Step 3—Life Exploration

Point out that James 4:4 alludes to the idea of trying to mix two unmixable substances—love for God and love for the world. Read James 4:8, emphasizing the term "double-minded." Ask, **What do you think "friendship with the world" means? Why do you think a person cannot be a friend to the ideals and values of the world and God at the same time? What does it mean to be double-minded? Are Christians to avoid non-Christians or anything un-Christian? Why or why not?**

Step 4—Conclusion

Give everyone a chance to silently and privately ask God to help them develop a real love for Him instead of the world.

Give each student a copy of "The Carnival of Life" booklet. Have students keep their booklets with them throughout the week to remind them to compare what they see in the world around them to tinsel and bright lights. Close in prayer.

YOU HAVE BEEN BORN INTO THE **CARNIVAL OF LIFE**.

SOME OF THE "RIDES" ARE EXCITING. SOME OF THE "GAMES" ARE FUN. BUT COMPARED TO **KINGDOM OF HEAVEN**, THIS WORLD IS NOTHING BUT TINSEL AND BRIGHT LIGHTS. TINSEL THAT RUSTS AND BRIGHT LIGHTS THAT FADE.

DON'T LET THIS WORLD SUCKER YOU. GIVE YOUR LIFE TO **JESUS**. HE WANTS YOU TO HAVE A GREAT LIFE ON EARTH AND FOREVER IN HEAVEN!

The CARNIVAL of LIFE
TOM FINLEY

HEY, OLD MAN! THIS CARNIVAL OF LIFE LOOKS FUN! HOW MUCH DOES IT COST TO GET IN?
IT COSTS NOTHING TO GET IN, KID. BUT IT'LL COST EVERYTHING YOU'VE GOT TO GET OUT.
END OF THE LINE
CANDY

OOPS! BOY, THIS CARNIVAL OF LIFE ROLLER COASTER SURE HAS ITS UPS AND DOWNS!
RAT RACE
ZOW!

OH— I THINK I'M GONNA BE SICK!
POP!

MAD HOUS

2

YOU HAVE BEEN BORN INTO THE **CARNIVAL OF LIFE**.

SOME OF THE "RIDES" ARE EXCITING. SOME OF THE "GAMES" ARE FUN. BUT COMPARED TO **KINGDOM OF HEAVEN**, THIS WORLD IS NOTHING BUT TINSEL AND BRIGHT LIGHTS. TINSEL THAT RUSTS AND BRIGHT LIGHTS THAT FADE.

DON'T LET THIS WORLD SUCKER YOU. GIVE YOUR LIFE TO **JESUS**, HE WANTS YOU TO HAVE A GREAT LIFE ON EARTH AND FOREVER IN HEAVEN!

11

4

9

6

7

The Hard (Hat) Truth

Focus of the Lesson: Hold on to Jesus for life.
Biblical Basis: John 18:28—19:16
Materials Needed: Copies of "The Hard (Hat) Truth" booklet, chalkboard and chalk, poster board, felt-tip pens.

Step 1—Approach to the Word

Draw on a chalkboard or describe several things that are important to hold on to, and ask students to tell what happens if you don't: the steering wheel of a fast moving car, the football that's been thrown to you in the end zone, the pitcher of root beer you are pouring into your boy- or girlfriend's glass, the hot pizza you're passing to him or her.

Say, **Some things are very important to hold on to! Today we are going to look at something that a Christian must hold on to at all costs.**

Step 2—Bible Exploration

Have students read "The Hard (Hat) Truth" booklet. Discuss the three passages found in the booklet, especially John 8:31,32. Say, **Jesus is the truth! What do you think happens to the person who doesn't hold on to Him?**

Explain that the class is now going to look at Pontius Pilate, a man who rejected Jesus even though he knew Him to be true. The background of the passage (John 18:28—19:16) is Jesus' trial just before His crucifixion. Have class form groups of three or four students. Give each group a section of the passage to read and report (for example, 18:28-32,33-37,38-40; 19:1-9,10-16).

Point out that there seems to be no question in Pilate's mind that Jesus was innocent of any criminal act. Yet Pilate chose to reject Jesus. Pilate was oh-so-close to heaven but missed it. Had he held on to the truth, he would be jumping for joy in heaven today. Someone else would have had to order Jesus' execution for our sins!

Step 3—Life Exploration

Allow your students to predict what will happen to the people in the following case studies. (Option: Small groups can create a skit around each case study.)

Jackie came to a great youth group meeting last month where she made a heartfelt decision for Christ. Since then, she hasn't followed up on her decision. She doesn't attend any Christian events, nor does she read her Bible.

For a long time Dwight has been praying that his mom would become a Christian. He intends to keep it up as long as necessary.

Jenna has been faithfully involved in your youth group for two years. She has just decided to go out with a guy who isn't a Christian.

Doctor Meyers is a psychology instructor at the local university. She is conducting a controlled experiment. She has asked 10 Christians to read their Bibles and pray every day and worship at church once a week. Another 10 Christians have been asked to read their Bibles and pray every day and worship once a month. The final 10 Christians are to never pray, read or worship. After six months, what do you think her findings will be?

Step 4—Conclusion

Option: Have students work individually to rate themselves in several important categories, such as time spent reading the Bible, minutes in prayer and so forth. For example, say **If you read the Bible once a day on average, give yourself 10 points. Once a week earns 5 points. Never is zero.**

After passing out the poster board and felt-tip pens, have the class work together to create a chart of what it feels is a reasonable time commitment in these areas: Bible study, church attendance, youth group activities, telling others about Christ, private prayer, reading Christian books and so forth.

Have those who are willing to abide by the chart sign it. Close in prayer.

"SHOW ME YOUR WAYS, O LORD, TEACH ME YOUR PATHS; GUIDE ME IN YOUR TRUTH AND TEACH ME, FOR YOU ARE GOD MY SAVIOR, AND MY HOPE IS IN YOU ALL DAY LONG" (PSALM 25:4,5).

"IF YOU HOLD TO MY TEACHING, YOU ARE REALLY MY DISCIPLES. THEN YOU WILL KNOW THE TRUTH, AND THE TRUTH WILL SET YOU FREE" (JOHN 8:31,32).

"I AM THE WAY AND THE TRUTH AND THE LIFE. NO ONE COMES TO THE FATHER EXCEPT THROUGH ME" (JOHN 14:6).

11

THE HARD (HAT) TRUTH
TOM FINLEY

WHAT?!?
WAAAAH!!

10

DO YOU BELIEVE IN GOD, CHIEF?
I SURE DO!

3

IF A PERSON GETS TOLD ABOUT JESUS EVERY WEEK BUT NEVER EXPERIENCES HIM PERSONALLY, WELL... THAT FAITH MAY NOT LAST EITHER. THAT'S WHY I'M WORRIED.

8

JESUS CHRIST DEMANDS COMMITMENT, A LIFE-CHANGING BELIEF IN HIM BECAUSE HE IS THE ABSOLUTE TRUTH.
BUT MANY PEOPLE HAVE NEVER EXPERIENCED THAT LIFE-CHANGING BELIEF. INSTEAD, THEY ONLY HAVE A THIN "COATING" OF CHRISTIANITY BECAUSE THEIR PARENTS MAKE THEM GO TO BIBLE STUDY EVERY WEEK OR THEY ATTEND CHURCH MEETINGS OUT OF HABIT. THESE THINGS ARE IMPORTANT, OF COURSE, BUT THEY ARE NO SUBSTITUTE FOR KNOWING JESUS CHRIST PERSONALLY.

5

YUM — THANK GOD I'M MARRIED TO A GREAT COOK!

2

BUT I'M WORRIED THAT SOME PEOPLE MAY BELIEVE IN JESUS CHRIST IN THE SAME WAY SOME PEOPLE BELIEVE IN SANTA CLAUS. MAYBE EVEN SOME OF THE PEOPLE READING THIS LITTLE BOOKLET!
?
WHAT'S THIS ABOUT SANTA CLAUS, CHIEF?

4

BUT WHAT'S THIS GOT TO DO WITH SANTIE?

6

"SHOW ME YOUR WAYS, O LORD, TEACH ME YOUR PATHS; GUIDE ME IN YOUR TRUTH AND TEACH ME, FOR YOU ARE GOD MY SAVIOR, AND MY HOPE IS IN YOU ALL DAY LONG"
(PSALM 25:4,5).

"IF YOU HOLD TO MY TEACHING, YOU ARE REALLY MY DISCIPLES. THEN YOU WILL KNOW THE TRUTH, AND THE TRUTH WILL SET YOU FREE"
(JOHN 8:31,32).

"I AM THE WAY AND THE TRUTH AND THE LIFE. NO ONE COMES TO THE FATHER EXCEPT THROUGH ME"
(JOHN 14:6).

11

THE POINT, OF COURSE, IS THAT JESUS IS TRUE AND CAN THEREFORE BE EXPERIENCED. SANTA CLAUS IS JUST A MYTH.
ANY IDIOT KNOWS THAT

9

KIDS BELIEVE IN SANTA CLAUS BECAUSE THEIR PARENTS TELL THEM TO, BUT THE CHILDREN NEVER EXPERIENCE ACTIVE, DYNAMIC RELATIONSHIPS WITH MR. CLAUS.
SO WHEN THEY GROW UP, THAT FAITH DISAPPEARS LIKE SMOKE IN THE WIND.

7

In the Light

Focus of the Lesson: Jesus is the light of the world, and we are, too.
Biblical Basis: Matthew 5:14-16; John 8:12
Materials Needed: Copies of the "In the Light" booklet, a flashlight, chalkboard and chalk, an infrared remote control.

Step 1—Approach to the Word

Show everyone a flashlight. Ask **When is this used? Why do we need it?** Have a few students describe their scariest moments in the dark. If a member of your church is blind, invite that person to share what it is like always to be in the dark.

Tell students that this lesson centers on Jesus being the light that chases away spiritual darkness. You'll also look at Jesus' statement that we Christians are the light of the world.

Step 2—Bible Exploration

Let everyone have and read a copy of the "In the Light" booklet. On the chalkboard write two headings: "The Flashlight" and "Jesus, the Light of the World." Using the Scripture and thoughts on page 11 of the booklet, discuss with your class the nature of the light from the flashlight and light from Jesus. Ask **What sort of things do the two lights reveal? In what ways can the two lights help guide us? What happens when the lights are missing in our lives?** Write students' responses under the appropriate headings.

Have your class form groups of three or four students. Have students read Matthew 5:14-16. Have them discuss the following questions: What does Jesus say we are? How does our light compare to the list on the chalkboard? What will happen if we shine our light as Jesus said?

Step 3—Life Exploration

Point out that Christians are the only true light that God shines in your community. Your young people have "ins" to areas where few adults can go, such as school and groups of peers. Have students suggest actual places and situations they can get into that adults would have a hard time entering.

In small groups or as an entire class, discuss practical ways (things young people could and would really do) to shine the light in some or all the places and situations they suggested, plus any of the following you have time for: the school newspaper, English class, a group of friends, the family dinner table, on a date and at a fun group event.

Step 4—Conclusion

Show your class the infrared remote control. Point it at the room and push a button or two. Ask if there is anyone who can explain how the remote control communicates with a television set. (The remote control uses a form of light called infrared, which humans cannot see.) Explain that the infrared light from the remote control is very bright. When you pushed the button, the light brightly lights up the whole room, but since we can't see it, we don't take any notice.

Encourage students to pray silently that God would give them and the people they are concerned about spiritual eyes sensitive to the light He shines on us.

THE LIGHT REVEALED THE TRUTH: HIGH-CLASS RESTAURANTS HAVE HIGH-CLASS ROACHES!

THE LORD JESUS CALLED HIMSELF THE LIGHT OF THIS WORLD:

"WHEN JESUS SPOKE AGAIN TO THE PEOPLE, HE SAID, 'I AM THE LIGHT OF THE WORLD. WHOEVER FOLLOWS ME WILL NEVER WALK IN DARKNESS, BUT WILL HAVE THE LIGHT OF LIFE.'" (JOHN 8:12).

HIS LIGHT REVEALS THE HIDDEN THINGS. HIS LIGHT CAN REVEAL OUR NEEDS FOR HIM. HIS LIGHT CAN GUIDE US THROUGH THE DARKNESS OF THIS WORLD TO THE BRIGHTNESS OF THE NEXT.

WHEN THINGS SEEM DIM AND YOU DON'T KNOW WHICH WAY TO GO—LET THE LIGHT IN.

IN THE LIGHT
TOM FINLEY

10

NOT LONG AGO I WAS CONTACTED BY A LOCAL RESTAURANT MANAGER. HIS ESTABLISHMENT HAD RECEIVED SEVERAL COMPLAINTS BY CUSTOMERS ABOUT COCKROACHES. HE WANTED ME TO PROVE ONCE AND FOR ALL THAT HIS HIGH-CLASS RESTAURANT HAD NO LOW-CLASS BUGS.

3

THROUGH CAREFUL SCIENTIFIC RESEARCH IN MY CRIME LAB, I HAD DISCOVERED A SURE-FIRE CALL TO ATTRACT ANY COCKROACHES IN THE BUILDING.
HERE, COCKROACHES! HERE, COCKROACHES!

8

COCKROACHES COME OUT IN THE DARK. THEREFORE, I ENTERED THE EMPTY RESTAURANT AT MIDNIGHT. I WAS USING MY HEAD.
KONK!
OUCH!

5

2

THE **LIGHT** REVEALED THE TRUTH: HIGH-CLASS RESTAURANTS HAVE **HIGH-CLASS ROACHES!**

THE **LORD JESUS** CALLED HIMSELF THE **LIGHT** OF THIS WORLD:

"WHEN JESUS SPOKE AGAIN TO THE PEOPLE, HE SAID, 'I AM THE LIGHT OF THE WORLD. WHOEVER FOLLOWS ME WILL NEVER WALK IN DARKNESS, BUT WILL HAVE THE LIGHT OF LIFE.'" (JOHN 8:12).

HIS LIGHT REVEALS THE HIDDEN THINGS. HIS LIGHT CAN REVEAL OUR NEEDS FOR HIM. HIS LIGHT CAN GUIDE US THROUGH THE DARKNESS OF THIS WORLD TO THE BRIGHTNESS OF THE NEXT.

WHEN THINGS SEEM DIM AND YOU DON'T KNOW WHICH WAY TO GO—LET THE LIGHT IN.

11

4

SUDDENLY I SPRANG TO THE WALL SWITCH. THE ELEMENT OF SURPRISE IS **VITAL!**

HERE, WALL SWITCH! HERE, WALL SWITCH!

NUTS.

AT LAST I FOUND IT. I CLICKED IT ON.

9

6

7

Just Be Yourself

Focus of the Lesson: Be yourself because you are God's masterpiece.
Biblical Basis: Genesis 1:27,31; Psalm 8:3-8; 139:14; Matthew 10:29-31; John 3:16; 2 Corinthians 5:17; Ephesians 1:3; 2:10; 1 John 3:1
Materials Needed: Copies of the "Just Be Yourself" booklet, slips of paper, pencils, a hat or other container for slips of paper.

Step 1—Approach to the Word

As you launch into this lesson, have all the students write their names on slips of paper that are placed in a hat or other container for use later in the lesson.

Ask your students to help you identify the highest-quality product in a number of categories that interest them: cars, dirt bikes, athletic equipment, fast food, stereos and the like. Ask students to tell why they picked the brands they did.

Say, **Obviously, some products set the pace for high standards. In the same way, God made all of us to the highest standards. You are His quality workmanship. You are God's masterpiece!**

Step 2—Bible Exploration

Conduct a mock trial with your students. Select one volunteer to be the defendant. Explain that the defendant has been accused of being a "mere low-quality human being of no real value." (You'll want a volunteer with a good self-image.)

You are the prosecutor. You will bring the charge against the defendant.

The defendant is being defended by a "dream team" of high-powered lawyers. The dream team is made up of all the students in your class formed into groups of three or four students. Give each group one or two of the passages in the Biblical Basis. These Scripture verses are the evidence the lawyers use to prove that the defendant is indeed a person of great value and quality.

The trial should proceed in this fashion:

First, the volunteer is selected and seated at the front of the class. Then the groups meet to examine their passages and to be sure they understand how those passages prove a person has great value and quality in God's eyes. When the trial begins, read the charge. Each group then presents its case for the defense. As they do, discuss the significance of each passage. Since you are the prosecution, you may want to say, **Do you mean to tell me that God calls us His workmanship—His masterpiece? Wow, score one point for your side!**

After all the evidence is presented, throw your hands up in mock frustration and declare that the defendant is free to go; he or she indeed is a high-quality masterpiece put together by God Himself.

Step 3—Life Exploration

Give each student a copy of the "Just Be Yourself" booklet to read. Lead a discussion by asking, **Is it common that young people today pretend they are something they are not? What are some of the ways young people do this? What might be some differences in the self-image of a person who pretends to be what he or she is not and the self-image of a person who strives to become better? How might it help a person to know that he or she is valued by God and is a work of art that God is crafting?**

Read the following case studies to your students, asking them to explain how they would respond to each person using wisdom from the Scriptures and discussions of today's lesson.

Katrina always seems to be down on herself. What uplifting encouragement would you give her?

Jeremy tells you that, even though he prays, God seems distant and uncaring.

Shannon is doing a school report on the foolishness of racism. What did you learn from today's class that Shannon could use in her report?

Step 4—Conclusion

Tell students to think silently of their favorite friends or family members, people they admire and respect. With that person in mind, each student is to create a simple card that gives at least five reasons from today's lesson why he or she is a valuable, quality masterpiece.

Collect all the cards. Draw one name from the container you filled at the beginning of the lesson. Give all the cards to that one person, reading them quickly as you do so. Your class will probably have a good time watching the embarrassed student hear the multitudes of uplifting comments —even if they weren't meant for him or her!

Encourage students to consciously look for people this week that they can uplift with the truths of today's lesson. Close in prayer.

JUST BE YOURSELF
DO I HAVE TO?
TOM FINLEY

HIS FACE WAS IN THE CARDBOARD BOX BEFORE HIM. HE REACHED IN, REMOVING A BLUE EYEBALL.

HE PRESSED THE EYE INTO THE FLESH OF HIS HEAD, THEN DID THE SAME WITH HIS OTHER EYE, MAKING SURE BOTH WERE LEVEL.
NOW HE COULD SEE HIS IMAGE IN THE MIRROR.
HE CHECKED HIS WATCH. ALMOST TIME TO GO.

HE TOOK HIS EARS FROM THE BOX AND SHOVED THEM INTO HIS SKULL, ONE ON EACH SIDE.
HE COULD DETECT THE BEAT FROM A RADIO IN AN APARTMENT DOWN THE HALL.

HE CHOSE A MOUTH, PREFERRING THE LARGER OF THE TWO. HE STUCK IT IN THE AREA JUST ABOVE HIS CHIN, MAKING SURE IT WAS IN THE SMILE POSITION, NOT THE FROWN.

A SMALL MASCULINE NOSE COMPLETED HIS IMAGE.

A HAT TOPPED OFF HIS HAIRLESS HEAD AND HE WAS READY TO JUMP IN HIS OLD CAR AND CRUISE.

MR. POTATO HEAD WAS SET TO GO!

THAT'S PRONOUNCED PAT-WAH HEAD, BOY. IT'S FRENCH!
GET AWAY, BOY. YA BOTHER ME.

TRY AS HE MIGHT, MR. "PAT-WAH" HEAD WILL ALWAYS BE JUST A POTATO IN DISGUISE.
HEY! WATCH OUT! ARE YOU CRAZY?

PEOPLE SOMETIMES TRY TO BE SOMETHING THEY ARE NOT. SOMETIMES IT WORKS FOR AWHILE, USUALLY NOT. IT'S LIKE A POTATO TRYING TO LOOK LIKE A HUMAN BEING. IT MIGHT FOOL OTHER POTATOES, BUT NOT THE HUMANS!
THE BEST BET IS TO SIMPLY BE YOURSELF.
FRENCH FRIES, ANYONE?
FRENCH FRIES?!? OH, NOooooooo

JUST BE YOURSELF
DO I HAVE TO?
TOM FINLEY

TRY AS HE MIGHT, MR. "PAT-WAH" HEAD WILL ALWAYS BE JUST A POTATO IN DISGUISE.
HEY! WATCH OUT! ARE YOU CRAZY?

10

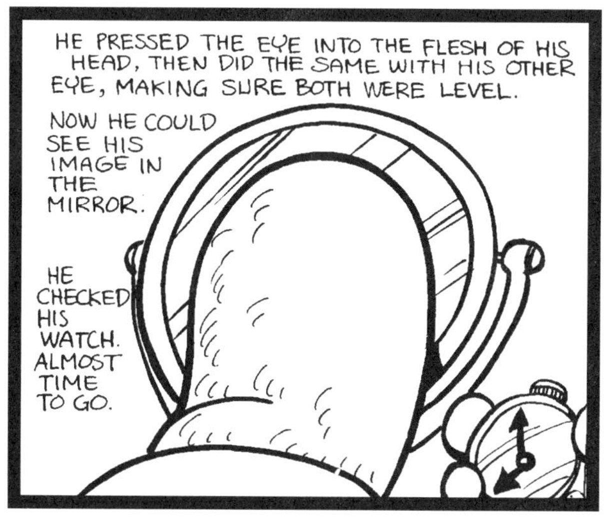

HE PRESSED THE EYE INTO THE FLESH OF HIS HEAD, THEN DID THE SAME WITH HIS OTHER EYE, MAKING SURE BOTH WERE LEVEL.
NOW HE COULD SEE HIS IMAGE IN THE MIRROR.
HE CHECKED HIS WATCH. ALMOST TIME TO GO.

3

MR. POTATO HEAD WAS SET TO GO!

8

HE CHOSE A MOUTH, PREFERRING THE LARGER OF THE TWO. HE STUCK IT IN THE AREA JUST ABOVE HIS CHIN, MAKING SURE IT WAS IN THE SMILE POSITION, NOT THE FROWN.

5

HIS FACE WAS IN THE CARDBOARD BOX BEFORE HIM. HE REACHED IN, REMOVING A BLUE EYEBALL.
2

PEOPLE SOMETIMES TRY TO BE SOMETHING THEY ARE NOT. SOMETIMES IT WORKS FOR AWHILE, USUALLY NOT. IT'S LIKE A POTATO TRYING TO LOOK LIKE A HUMAN BEING. IT MIGHT FOOL OTHER POTATOES, BUT NOT THE HUMANS!
THE BEST BET IS TO SIMPLY BE YOURSELF.
FRENCH FRIES, ANYONE?
FRENCH FRIES?!? OH, NOOooooo
11

HE TOOK HIS EARS FROM THE BOX AND SHOVED THEM INTO HIS SKULL, ONE ON EACH SIDE.
HE COULD DETECT THE BEAT FROM A RADIO IN AN APARTMENT DOWN THE HALL.
4

THAT'S PRONOUNCED PAT-WAH HEAD, BOY. IT'S FRENCH!
GET AWAY, BOY. YA BOTHER ME.
9

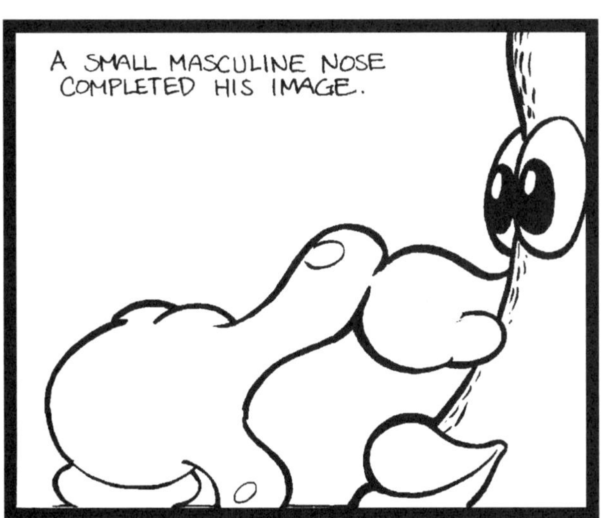

A SMALL MASCULINE NOSE COMPLETED HIS IMAGE.
6

A HAT TOPPED OFF HIS HAIRLESS HEAD AND HE WAS READY TO JUMP IN HIS OLD CAR AND CRUISE.
7

The Master Deceiver

Focus of the Lesson: Satan is the master deceiver. Don't be fooled.
Biblical Basis: John 8:44; 17:15; 1 Peter 5:8,9; 1 John 5:4,5
Materials Needed: Copies of "The Master Deceiver" booklet, chalkboard and chalk, index cards, thumbtacks or tape, a carrot on a stick, pencils.

Step 1—Approach to the Word

Give each student a copy of "The Master Deceiver" booklet. Instruct them to read only to page 9. At that point, let the class try to guess how Houdini performed his trick.

Read the rest of the booklet to your class. Say, **Here is something to think about. Like those who fell for Houdini's tricks, many people have been fooled into accepting the lies of Satan, the master deceiver. He wants to fool us too, so let's see if we can come up with a way to fool him!**

Step 2—Bible Exploration

On the chalkboard write these four headings: "John 8:44—Jesus talking to antagonistic Jews"; "John 17:15—Jesus praying to God about Christians"; "1 Peter 5:8,9—Peter writing to Christians"; " 1 John 5:4,5—John writing to Christians."

Have your class form groups of three or four students. Assign each passage to a group, telling students to summarize and report. Discuss what students have found and write the highlights under each column. The main points are that Satan is a liar and murderer, God protects us from Satan, we must be alert and self-controlled as we resist the devil and stand firm, and faith in Jesus insures our safety.

Point out that the biblical secret to staying out of the lion's jaws is to stick close to God.

Step 3—Life Exploration

Ask your students to think about some of the evidence they see for Satan's attack on this world, especially against people their age. Have each student write one piece of evidence on an index card. Some of the things students write about might be violence in the home or at school, drugs, anti-Christian attitudes at school and so forth. Collect the cards, shuffle them and draw them one at a time to discuss.

As you discuss each suggestion, ask the class if everyone agrees that Satan is involved in that particular item. Ask, **How much danger does it represent to the average teen and to society? Is it hard or easy for the average young Christian to stay away from? Also discuss any positive response Christians could make against each item. Ask, What could the Christian do? What ammunition does God supply?** Talk about how being alert and self-controlled fits in with each item.

Distribute more index cards. Have students work in pairs to write short pithy responses to Satan's attacks. The statements can be anything from "Pray about it!" to "Hang in there with your Christian friends!" to "Don't listen to his lies!" Scripture verses would be good, too. Collect cards and tack them to a bulletin board or tape them to a poster on the wall.

Step 4—Conclusion

Show your students a carrot on a stick. Say, **It's easy to resist Satan in our cozy classroom. But you have to go out and face his attacks and temptations all around you. I want you to remember this carrot on a stick. Satan dangles carrots like this in front of our noses, the way old-timers used to dangle them in front of mules to get the mules to do their bidding. Don't be fooled. The things Satan offers may look good, but he will lead you in the totally wrong direction.**

Eat the carrot, then have volunteers close in prayer.

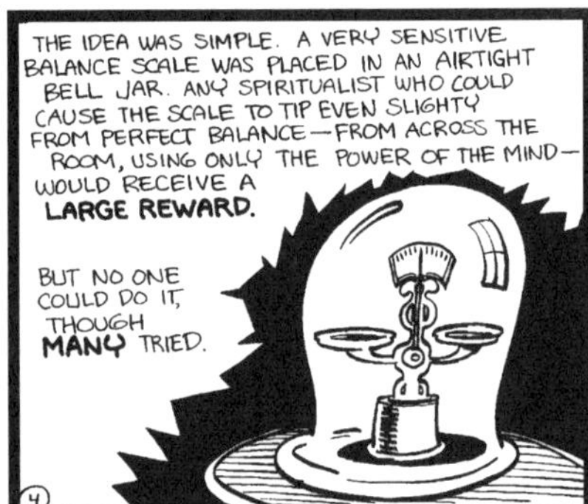

HERE'S SOMETHING TO THINK ABOUT:

SATAN IS THE ABSOLUTE **MASTER DECEIVER** AND HE IS STILL UP TO HIS OLD TRICKS. ONCE, WHEN HE WAS TRYING TO TEMPT **JESUS**, SATAN OFFERED JESUS THE **WHOLE WORLD**: "IF YOU WORSHIP ME, IT WILL ALL BE YOURS" (LUKE 4:7). JESUS DIDN'T BITE, OF COURSE. AS JESUS SAID LATER, "WHEN HE LIES, HE SPEAKS HIS NATIVE LANGUAGE, FOR HE IS A LIAR AND THE FATHER OF LIES" (JOHN 8:44).

DON'T BE FOOLED! SATAN WILL OFFER YOU THIS WORLD, BUT IT'S A **SORRY** SUBSTITUTE FOR THE **NEXT** WORLD— THE ONE ONLY GOD CAN GIVE.

THE MASTER DECEIVER
BY TOM FINLEY

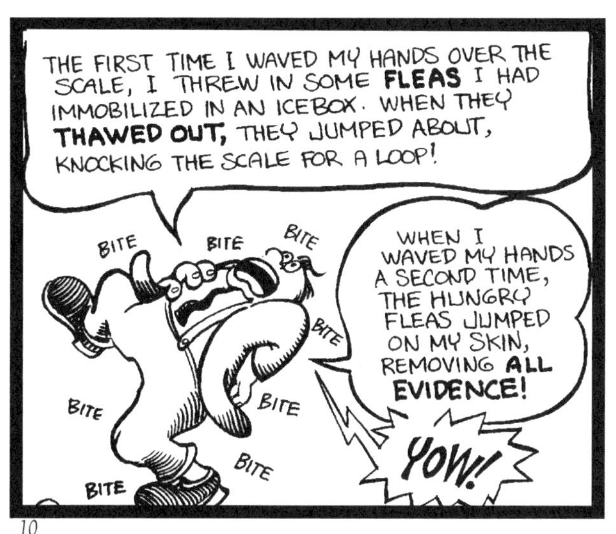

THE FIRST TIME I WAVED MY HANDS OVER THE SCALE, I THREW IN SOME FLEAS I HAD IMMOBILIZED IN AN ICEBOX. WHEN THEY THAWED OUT, THEY JUMPED ABOUT, KNOCKING THE SCALE FOR A LOOP!
WHEN I WAVED MY HANDS A SECOND TIME, THE HUNGRY FLEAS JUMPED ON MY SKIN, REMOVING ALL EVIDENCE!
BITE
BITE
BITE
BITE
BITE
BITE
BITE
BITE
YOW!!

10

THE FAMOUS ILLUSIONIST AND ESCAPE ARTIST HARRY HOUDINI LOVED TO EXPOSE THESE PEOPLE AS FRAUDS. BUT HE DIDN'T MIND HAVING A BIT OF FUN PERFORMING HIS OWN "MIRACLES." HERE'S ONE SUCH EVENT.
THIS JUST IN! A GROUP OF ESTEEMED SCIENTISTS HAS ISSUED A CHALLENGE TO ALL SPIRITUALISTS TO PROVE THEIR CLAIMS!
WCBS RADIO

3

FOR SOME TIME THEY EXAMINED THE DEVICE CLOSELY. NO SIGN OF TAMPERING COULD BE FOUND. AFTER CONSIDERING ALL THE ANGLES, THEY CONCLUDED THAT HOUDINI HAD INDEED LIFTED THE LID ON THE SPIRIT WORLD OR ON SOME FORM OF STRANGE MENTAL POWER.
HAND HIM THE BREAD, FRED.

8

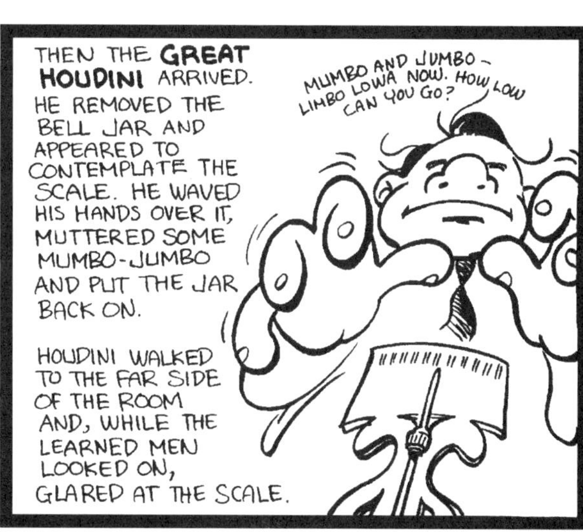

THEN THE GREAT HOUDINI ARRIVED. HE REMOVED THE BELL JAR AND APPEARED TO CONTEMPLATE THE SCALE. HE WAVED HIS HANDS OVER IT, MUTTERED SOME MUMBO-JUMBO AND PUT THE JAR BACK ON.
HOUDINI WALKED TO THE FAR SIDE OF THE ROOM AND, WHILE THE LEARNED MEN LOOKED ON, GLARED AT THE SCALE.
MUMBO AND JUMBO - LIMBO LOWA NOW. HOW LOW CAN YOU GO?

5

BACK IN THE EARLY PART OF THE TWENTIETH CENTURY, MANY PEOPLE BELIEVED IN AND CONSULTED **MEDIUMS** AND **SPIRITULISTS**— MEN AND WOMEN WHO CLAIMED TO BE IN CONTACT WITH DEPARTED SOULS, ABLE TO MOVE OBJECTS WITH THEIR MINDS AND SO FORTH.

EENIE MEENIE, CHILLY BEANIE, THE SPIRITS ARE ABOUT TO SPEAK!

MORE MONEY IS REQUIRED.

2

HERE'S SOMETHING TO THINK ABOUT:

SATAN IS THE ABSOLUTE **MASTER DECEIVER** AND HE IS STILL UP TO HIS OLD TRICKS. ONCE, WHEN HE WAS TRYING TO TEMPT **JESUS**, SATAN OFFERED JESUS THE **WHOLE WORLD**: "IF YOU WORSHIP ME, IT WILL ALL BE YOURS" (LUKE 4:7). JESUS DIDN'T BITE, OF COURSE. AS JESUS SAID LATER, "WHEN HE LIES, HE SPEAKS HIS NATIVE LANGUAGE, FOR HE IS A LIAR AND THE FATHER OF LIES" (JOHN 8:44).

DON'T BE FOOLED! SATAN WILL OFFER YOU THIS WORLD, BUT IT'S A SORRY SUBSTITUTE FOR THE **NEXT** WORLD— THE ONE ONLY GOD CAN GIVE.

11

THE IDEA WAS SIMPLE. A VERY SENSITIVE BALANCE SCALE WAS PLACED IN AN AIRTIGHT BELL JAR. ANY SPIRITUALIST WHO COULD CAUSE THE SCALE TO TIP EVEN SLIGHTY FROM PERFECT BALANCE—FROM ACROSS THE ROOM, USING ONLY THE POWER OF THE MIND— WOULD RECEIVE A **LARGE REWARD.**

BUT NO ONE COULD DO IT, THOUGH **MANY** TRIED.

4

BUT HARRY HAD **HOODWINKED** THEM. IT WAS SIMPLY AN INGENIOUS TRICK—SO HE DIDN'T TAKE THE MONEY!

CAN YOU GUESS HOW I DID IT?

GIVE IT A TRY!

9

6

7

Old Tired Yolks

Focus of the Lesson: Life is filled with choices—choose wisely.
Biblical Basis: Joshua 24:1-14
Materials Needed: Copies of the "Old Tired Yolks" booklets, chalkboard and chalk.

Step 1—Approach to the Word

Tell your students about the South American soccer player who accidentally scored a goal for the other team. Another player kicked the ball, it hit him on the head and deflected into the opponents' goal. His team lost the game and was eliminated from the World Cup play-offs. A few days later the player was murdered.

Say, **In soccer, basketball, football and other sports, the main idea is to score points by reaching a goal, but it has to be the right goal. In basketball, for instance, it's not enough to shoot at any basket; you have to choose the correct basket. You must pick one over the other. You can't have both. In life we often must pick one goal over another, one direction over another. Today we want to talk about how to do this wisely.**

Step 2—Bible Exploration

Distribute copies of the "Old Tired Yolks" booklet. Have students read them. Discuss the main point of the booklet—choosing either to live for God or to ignore Him rather than trying to have it both ways. Students should be aware that trying to mix strong Christian beliefs with a sin-filled life makes it impossible to enjoy either. (Ignoring God may seem enjoyable for a time, but the benefits are short-lived.)

Have your class form groups of three or four students. Have students read Joshua 24:1-14. Lead a class discussion focused on the choice Joshua gave the people. Ask, **Did Joshua give them the possibility of mixing the two choices? What do you suppose would have happened if they tried? Can you name some important issues that people your age struggle with—issues that involve choosing one direction over another?** (Write them on the chalkboard. Try to come up with at least five.) **Do most people your age try hard to choose right? Do many people avoid decisions and simply try to enjoy the best of all worlds? If so, why?**

Step 3—Life Exploration

Here are some wise tips regarding decision making. Write them on the chalkboard and discuss their significance:
    Always go God's way.
    Ask yourself which way is likely to bring the most honor to God.
    Does the Bible speak against a particular direction?
    What do wise Christians advise?
    Point out that these tips make it simpler to make decisions. Let the students discuss the following case studies:
    Judy and her two girlfriends are discussing boys. They've been told that it's O.K. to have sex with someone you truly love. Which side of the issue should they choose? (Have students use the list on the board as a basis for their discussion.)
    As Christians, Paul and his two pals have rightly decided to abstain from sex until marriage. However, they are wondering just how far a boy can go with a girl. How can they decide? (Again, have students use the list on the board. Note that this decision is harder to determine but can still be made with a good deal of confidence.)
    Use the list of issues on the chalkboard as a springboard to discussing wise decision making.

Step 4—Conclusion

Impress upon your class the importance and the joyous benefits of making correct godly decisions. Tell them, **I have one more key tip for you. A great way to make a wise decision and to stick with it is to make it with someone else. Some people call this accountability; some call it joining a support group. Let's spend the rest of the class time building our own support group so that we can help each other choose wisely in life.**

Have students come up with godly commitments they want to make and a simple contract to sign. Let them exchange phone numbers and agree to call each other on a regular basis for support and prayer.

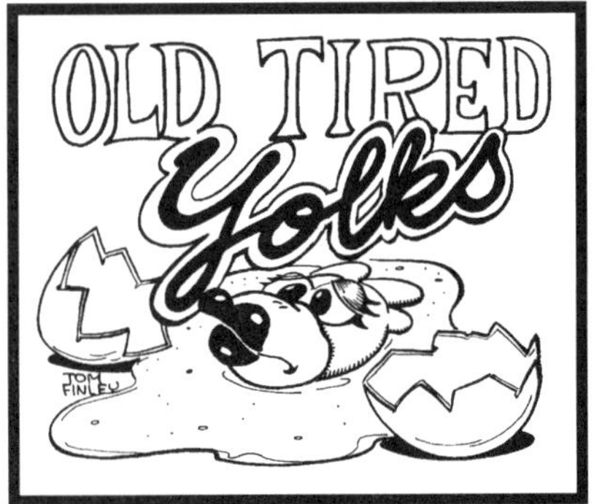

THE OLD MEN IN THE TRUCK PUT AN END TO THELMA THE CHICKEN'S INDECISION.

SOONER OR LATER EACH AND EVERY PERSON MUST DECIDE WHAT TO DO WITH **JESUS**, WHETHER TO STAY ON THE SIDE OF THE ROAD AND IGNORE HIM, OR TO CROSS THE ROAD AND LOVE AND FOLLOW HIM!

UNFORTUNATELY, MANY CHICKENS—ER, PEOPLE, I MEAN—TRY TO SIT IN THE MIDDLE OF THE ROAD ENJOYING BOTH WORLDS.

IT'S GOT TO BE EITHER ONE OR THE OTHER. FOLLOW JESUS WHOLEHEARTEDLY, OR IGNORE HIM TOTALLY. OTHERWISE YOU END UP LIKE THELMA, ENJOYING NOTHING.

CHOOSE, IF YOU HAVEN'T ALREADY, WHICH SIDE OF THE ROAD YOU WANT TO BE ON!

DON'T BE A DUMB CLUCK!

 © 1995 by Gospel Light. Permission to photocopy granted.

Thelma used to crow country tunes down at the chicken shack panel:

Thelma runs across the road panel:

ONCE UPON A TIME THERE WAS A CHICKEN. IT MUST HAVE BEEN A GIRL CHICKEN, SINCE TO MY KNOWLEDGE THERE IS NO SUCH THING AS A GUY CHICKEN.
HER NAME WAS THELMA—THELMA THE CHICKEN.

2

ONE DAY THELMA THE CHICKEN DECIDED TO CROSS THE ROAD. WHY, YOU MAY ASK, DID THE CHICKEN CROSS...
OH, NO YOU DON'T! I AIN'T FALLING FOR THAT OLD JOKE!

4

WELL, TO MAKE A LONG CHICKEN SHORT...
SLISH
!!!

9

SAY, BURT. DID YOU HEAR ABOUT THE TWO FARMERS THAT RAN OVER THE HENWAY?
WHAT'S A HENWAY?
OH, ABOUT EIGHT POUNDS!
OWLS ARE SMARTER THAN CHICKENS, YOU KNOW.
REALLY?
HAVE YOU EVER HEARD OF KENTUCKY FRIED OWL?
ACME FARMS

6

IF A ROOSTER LAYS AN EGG ON THE TOP OF A PITCHED ROOF, WHICH WAY DOES THE EGG ROLL?
ROOSTERS DON'T LAY EGG ROLLS!

7

One Big Place

Focus of the Lesson: Worship the Creator.
Biblical Basis: Psalm 19:1; Acts 4:24; 17:24-28; Romans 1:20; Revelation 4:11
Materials Needed: Copies of the "One Big Place" booklet, chalkboard and chalk, materials to make a large banner as described in the Life Exploration section. If you wish to celebrate communion, provide the necessary elements.
Before Class: This session centers on a worship service in the classroom. You'll want someone to come prepared to lead the group in singing.

Step 1—Approach to the Word

Distribute copies of the "One Big Place" booklet for students to read. Tell your class, **Our God is indeed one great God! We are going to look in the Bible at just a few of the many wonderful reasons to love and worship Him. Then we will celebrate our God with a time of singing and praise.**

Step 2—Bible Exploration

Divide the students into five groups. Assign the Biblical Basis passages, one to each group. Each group is to come up with reasons to praise God, as found in its passage. These reasons include His awesome glory, His eternal power and divine nature, the fact that He made everything, and the fact that He orders our lives in such a way as to bring us to salvation.

As students share what they've discovered, write their thoughts on the chalkboard. Add any other reasons to praise God that students might suggest.

Step 3—Life Exploration

Roll out a long sheet of paper across a couple of tables. Provide whatever students need to make a banner that spells out Psalm 19:1—paint, markers, pastels, spray glitter and the like. Encourage the students to add stars and other symbols of God's great creative power. When finished, display the banner on the wall.

Conduct a youth worship service. We suggest that you intersperse group singing with prayers of praise and moments for students to share what God means to them. It would be good for students to thank God for each other.

If you wish, conduct a communion service near the end of the hour. Check with your minister to be sure everything is done in proper fashion.

Step 4—Conclusion

Lead a closing prayer of thanksgiving. Quote Jude 24,25: **"To him who is able to keep you from falling and to present you before his glorious presence without fault and with great joy—to the only God our Savior be glory, majesty, power and authority, through Jesus Christ our Lord, before all ages, now and forevermore! Amen."**

LET'S FACE IT: THE UNIVERSE IS ONE BIG PLACE!

"THE HEAVENS DECLARE THE GLORY OF GOD; THE SKIES PROCLAIM THE WORK OF HIS HANDS" (PSALM 19:1).

OUR GOD IS A GREAT GOD!

Tom Finley
ONE
BIG
PLACE

THE TOTAL COST TO YOU IS...
GAA!
ACME GAS
COMPANY, INC.
$740, 000, 000,
000, 000, 000, 0
PLUS $1.50 ONE CAN OIL.
TOTAL: $74

10

OK, SEE IT? NOW POINT YOUR CAR AT THE MOON, SHIFT INTO LOW AND LIFT OFF.

3

ONWARD YOU PUSH, OUT TOWARD THE SEEMINGLY LIMITLESS GRANDEUR BEFORE YOU. ON TO THE CLOUDS OF MAGELLAN, OUR NEARBY GALACTIC NEIGHBOR. THE TRIP TAKES ABOUT 2,490,400,000,000 YEARS, GIVE OR TAKE A COUPLE OF MINUTES.
DISNEYLAND
NEIGHBOR GALAXY
MAP TO THE STARS
LIZ TAYLOR
JOHN WAYNE'S HOUSE

8

WAVE BYE-BYE AS YOU PUTT PAST THE MOON. NEXT STOP, MARS. YOUR CAR HAS BEEN GETTING 25 MILES TO THE GALLON OF GASOLINE. IT TOOK 9,554 GALLONS TO GET AS FAR AS LUNA. AT $1.35 PER GALLON, YOU'VE JUST BLOWN $12,898.

5

RUN OUTSIDE AND JUMP INTO YOUR CAR. FILL UP THE TANK AND TAKE A SACK LUNCH BECAUSE THIS IS GOING TO BE A **LONG** DRIVE. BUZZ AROUND UNTIL YOU CAN SEE THE MOON. (YOU MAY HAVE TO DRIVE TO THE OTHER SIDE OF THE PLANET.)

LET'S FACE IT: THE UNIVERSE IS ONE **BIG PLACE!**

"THE HEAVENS DECLARE THE GLORY OF GOD; THE SKIES PROCLAIM THE WORK OF HIS HANDS" (PSALM 19:1).

OUR GOD IS A GREAT GOD!

THE MOON IS ABOUT 238,857 MILES ABOVE YOUR HEAD. AT 55 MILES AN HOUR (YOU DON'T WANT TO BREAK THE SPEED LIMIT, YOU KNOW), THE MOON IS 4,343 HOURS AWAY. THAT'S 181 DAYS. IT WILL TAKE ABOUT A YEAR ROUND TRIP— EXCEPT YOU WON'T BE COMING BACK.

MOST SCIENTISTS AGREE THAT THIS IS WELL OVER **100 TIMES THE AGE OF THE UNIVERSE.** OH, WELL.

LET'S BE KIND. WE'LL SAY MARS IS ONLY 48,000,000 MILES AWAY RIGHT NOW. THAT'S ABOUT 219 YEARS DRIVE TIME. A BARGAIN AT LESS THAN $1,200,000.

ZOOM BY JUPITER AND THE REST OF THE PLANETS. ZERO IN ON THE NEAREST STAR—ALPHA PROXIMA— ONLY 460,000,000,000 HOURS AWAY, A MERE 52,000,000 YEARS. THE BILL IS NOW, ER...LET'S SEE... $11,500,000,000,000.

One Fine Day in Sunday School

Focus of the Lesson: We are to courageously answer Christ's call to live for Him.

Biblical Basis: Matthew 26:57-75; John 21:1-19; Romans 5:6; 8:3; 1 Thessalonians 5:10

Materials Needed: Copies of the "One Fine Day in Sunday School" booklet, a large sheet of paper, felt-tip pens, chalkboard and chalk.

Before class: Assemble a panel discussion group of two or three adults who have demonstrated a commitment to serving God at work or home.

Step 1—Approach to the Word

Hang on the wall a large sheet of paper labeled "Because Jesus Loves Me, I will...." As students enter the room, let them write their answers on the paper with a felt-tip pen. No two answers can be the same.

When ready to begin, comment on the answers, thanking everyone for their input. Explain that this lesson focuses on the courage it takes to live for Christ.

Step 2—Bible Exploration

Distribute copies of the "One Fine Day in Sunday School" booklet. After reading the story and the Bible passages it contains, students should be able to tell you that the main theme is living for Jesus because He died and now lives for us. The story also hints at the courage required to take a strong stand for Christ in the face of possible criticism from friends and even family.

Ask students to comment on living pure, godly lives in their world—is it relatively easy or does it cost them? Chances are, your students will feel that the price is not high. But they are likely to recognize that there are situations in which siding with God would be unpopular and costly. Talk about the courage and commitment it takes to stand publicly in favor of school prayer or against the use of condoms, to break through racial cliques on campus or to show genuine friendship to that one kid in school that everyone abuses.

Have your class form four groups. Assign one of the four Gospel passages found in the Biblical Basis to each group. Each group is to read its passage and report back to class.

Discuss Matthew 26:17-68 first. Ask, **Where was Peter in this passage? Why was he there?** (He was watching Jesus' trial, hoping to see the outcome.) Next focus on verses 69-75. Discuss the "courage level" Peter displays. (None.) **Why did he deny Christ?** John 21:1-14 comes next. **Was Peter taking a little vacation from God?** Finally, go over John 21:15-19. Discuss the nature of the call that Jesus gave Peter. **In verses 18 and 19, what evidence do we see that Peter heartily and courageously answered the call?**

Step 3—Life Exploration

Head up a panel discussion with two or three adults from your church who have answered God's call. Remember, God's calling extends not only to the pastor, but to the woman who works to raise godly children, the laborer who maintains a Christian life of integrity and the college student who believes God wants him or her to pursue journalism. Allow students to question each panelist regarding the commitment required, the resulting problems and blessings, and so forth.

Have panelists describe how they came to understand God's calling and what they had to do to prepare for it. What parts did prayer, church, Bible study, Christian friends and the like play in the successes they've enjoyed? Did it take courage to commit to God's calling? What were the costs involved? Write these answers in short form on the chalkboard.

Step 4—Conclusion

Let students pray about their commitments to live for Christ and His calling using the items on the chalkboard as a guide.

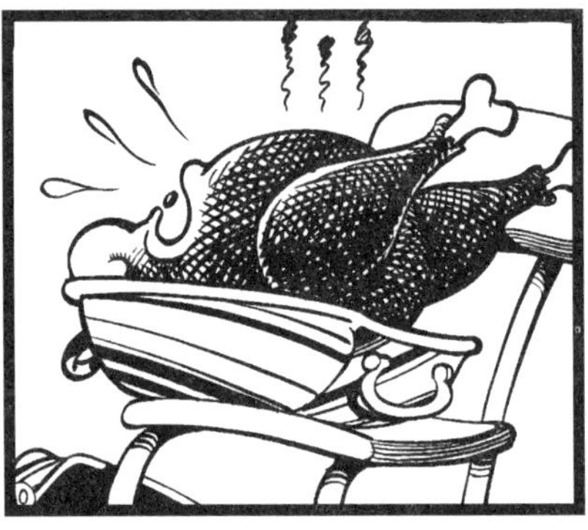

THE LORD JESUS CHRIST DIED SO THAT WE MAY LIVE!
CHECK OUT THESE GREAT TRUTHS:

"YOU SEE, AT JUST THE RIGHT TIME, WHEN WE WERE STILL POWERLESS, CHRIST DIED FOR THE UNGODLY" (ROMANS 5:6).

"CHRIST JESUS, WHO DIED — MORE THAN THAT, WHO WAS RAISED TO LIFE — IS AT THE RIGHT HAND OF GOD AND IS ALSO INTERCEDING FOR US" (ROMANS 8:34).

JESUS DIED FOR US. LET'S LIVE FOR HIM!

ONE FINE DAY IN SUNDAY SCHOOL
Tom Finley

THIS IS A WONDERFUL TRUTH! SADLY, SOME REFUSE TO BELIEVE JESUS DIED TO SHOW HIS LOVE FOR US.
THEY ARE LIKE OSTRICHES THAT HIDE FROM THE TRUTH BY STICKING THEIR HEADS IN THE SAND.
BOY, I'M GLAD I'M NOT LIKE ONE OF THEM!
POP!
HEY! WHAT?
UGH!
BONK!

SPIRITUALLY, THESE PEOPLE ARE DEAD DUCKS.

MAYBE SOME PEOPLE ARE CHICKEN TO RECOGNIZE THE TRUTH.
THEY ARE SPINELESS, LIKE JELLYFISH.
BROCK!
BROCK!

2

THE LORD JESUS CHRIST DIED SO THAT WE MAY LIVE!

CHECK OUT THESE GREAT TRUTHS:

"YOU SEE, AT JUST THE RIGHT TIME, WHEN WE WERE STILL POWERLESS, CHRIST DIED FOR THE UNGODLY" (ROMANS 5:6).

"CHRIST JESUS, WHO DIED — MORE THAN THAT, WHO WAS RAISED TO LIFE — IS AT THE RIGHT HAND OF GOD AND IS ALSO INTERCEDING FOR US " (ROMANS 8:34).

JESUS DIED FOR US. LET'S LIVE FOR HIM!

11

4

9

6

7

Power to Spare

Focus of the Lesson: The Christian's power for daily living is the Holy Spirit.

Biblical Basis: Acts 1:8; 17:1-9; 1 Corinthians 4:20; 2 Peter 1:3

Materials Needed: Copies of the "Power to Spare" booklet, chalkboard and chalk, a large sheet of paper, felt-tip pens. Optional: two long wood screws, two big blocks of wood, a hand screwdriver, a power drill with a screwdriver bit, eye protection for two people.

Step 1—Approach to the Word

Describe things that have power and ask students to explain what the power of each can do: a can of gasoline, a stick of dynamite, a mighty waterfall, a raging storm, an earthquake, a tsunami and so forth.

Optional Approach: Give the long wood screw and the screwdriver to one student. As the student starts to drive the screw into a block of wood, give another person a similar screw and the power drill with the screwdriver bit. It is a good safety precaution to provide eye protection for the volunteers. Be sure the wood block with the power drill is held securely. Have a race to see who can finish the job quickest and easiest. The power drill wins every time.

Say, **Today we talk about power. This power makes it possible for us to lead fulfilling, successful lives—the power of God.**

Step 2—Bible Exploration

Have your class form groups of three or four students. Have groups read Acts 17:1-9. Have each group create a radio or TV news drama centered on the events of the passage. Call one or two groups to perform their dramas.

Discuss what the students have done, then ask, **What message was Paul preaching to the citizens of Thessalonica? What was the response? What did the jealous Jews do? What do you suppose was meant when some said the Christians had "caused trouble all over the world"?**

The trouble was they were leading people to Jesus Christ. People were giving their lives to Jesus by the thousands. Society was being affected. Things weren't the same.

Make it clear that the Early Church enjoyed such rapid and widespread success because the power of God was at work in a dynamic fashion.

Give each student a copy of the "Power to Spare" booklet. When everyone has read the booklet, have students explain where the Christian's power comes from. Ask, **What one specific thing does Acts 1:8 say the power is for? What does 2 Peter 1:3 say about God's power in the Christian's life?** To help drive home the importance of the three Scripture passages in the booklet, have kids reword them as negatives ("But you will not receive power...you will not be my witnesses.").

Step 3—Life Exploration

Working with your students, make a list on the chalkboard of areas in which young people need God's power. List as many items as you can. To stimulate thinking, suggest broad areas by asking your students about home life, school, recreation, friends, inner thoughts, temptations young people face and so on.

Now check off each item on the list, discussing specific ways God's power could help a Christian do the right thing or succeed in some way. For instance, the power of God can help a Christian speak boldly and freely as a witness to non-Christian friends.

Ask students to work privately to come up with at least one area of life in which they feel frustrated and would like God to step in with His power. Ask for volunteers only to share their thoughts. Discuss frustrations or desires you have had in the past and ways in which you have seen God's power at work.

Step 4—Conclusion

Hang a large sheet of paper by the main exit door. As students leave, have them scrawl various graffiti-like statements about God's power.

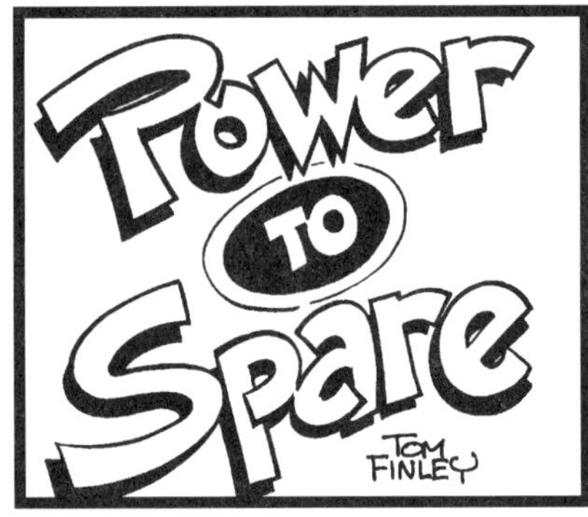

A CAR NEEDS GASOLINE. NO GAS, NO POWER. NO POWER, YOU GO NOWHERE.

IT'S JUST LIKE THAT WITH THE CHRISTIAN LIFE:

"BUT YOU WILL RECEIVE POWER WHEN THE HOLY SPIRIT COMES ON YOU; AND YOU WILL BE MY WITNESSES" (ACTS 1:8).

"FOR THE KINGDOM OF GOD IS NOT A MATTER OF TALK BUT OF POWER" (1 CORINTHIANS 4:20).

"HIS DIVINE POWER HAS GIVEN US EVERY-THING WE NEED FOR LIFE AND GODLINESS" (2 PETER 1:3).

GOD GIVES US **POWER** FOR DAILY LIVING! FILL UP WITH GOD. YOU WON'T RUN EMPTY!

Power
to
Spare
Tom Finley

BEEP!
sFLAT!
ACME HEAVY HAULERS
CRUNCH!
BUT I DIDN'T.

WELL, NOT TOO HOT.

HUFF!
PUFF!

...OUT OF GAS!

THE DOGBREATH GANG HAD JUST ROBBED THE BANK.
I WAS IN HOT PURSUIT.

A CAR NEEDS GASOLINE. NO GAS, NO POWER. NO POWER, YOU GO NOWHERE.
IT'S JUST LIKE THAT WITH THE CHRISTIAN LIFE:
"BUT YOU WILL RECEIVE POWER WHEN THE HOLY SPIRIT COMES ON YOU; AND YOU WILL BE MY WITNESSES" (ACTS 1:8).
"FOR THE KINGDOM OF GOD IS NOT A MATTER OF TALK BUT OF POWER" (1 CORINTHIANS 4:20).
"HIS DIVINE POWER HAS GIVEN US EVERYTHING WE NEED FOR LIFE AND GODLINESS" (2 PETER 1:3).
GOD GIVES US POWER FOR DAILY LIVING! FILL UP WITH GOD. YOU WON'T RUN EMPTY!

SUDDENLY...
POW!
POP!
KA-PUTT!

THE DOGBREATH GANG GOT AWAY,

GROAN

UGH!
OOGH!

Something Fishy

Focus of the Lesson: Be ready for the wonderful new world Christ has promised.

Biblical Basis: Luke 21:33; 2 Peter 3:10-13; Revelation 21:7

Materials Needed: Copies of the "Something Fishy" booklet, chalkboard and chalk, paper, pencils, felt-tip pens. Optional: candle, paper and firecracker (if legal in your area).

Step 1—Approach to the Word

Show the following objects to your class (or draw them on the chalkboard): a candle, a piece of crumpled paper and a firecracker. Say, **Let's have a vote. Pick the one that represents the way you think the world and society will end. Will it slowly melt down like this candle? Will it burn quickly like this paper? Or will it vaporize in one giant explosion like this firecracker? If you have a completely different idea, be sure to let us know.**

Tell your students that the Bible has much to say not only about how this world will end but what will rise from its ashes.

Step 2—Bible Exploration

Distribute copies of the "Something Fishy" booklet to your class. Ask students to read them and write quick paraphrases of the 2 Peter passage, which describes how the earth will end and how God will form the new one.

Have your class form groups of three or four students. Give each group paper and pencils or felt-tip pens. Instruct students to write newspaper articles on the Bible passages studied. Each group can work on a different aspect of the newspaper: articles, editorials, cartoons and photos. Discuss and display the results.

Compare 2 Peter 3:11,12 with students' paraphrases and newspapers. The key words to emphasize are holy and godly. Move on to the Bible Exploration by challenging students to help you think up a list of steps young Christians need to take in order to grow in holiness and godliness.

Step 3—Life Exploration

List the steps on the chalkboard under the heading "Gettin' Ready for God's New World." Encourage students' thinking by asking, **What are some things Christians do that please God? If a plant needs air, soil, sun and water to grow, what are some things Christians need in order to grow? What are some of the dangers young Christians must avoid?**

The list should include things like prayer, Bible study, worship, fellowship with other Christians, various temptations to avoid and so on. Read Revelation 21:7 from the last page of "Something Fishy" and discuss how overcoming relates to the list.

Step 4—Conclusion

Have students work in pairs to create a "Ticket to the Next World." Each ticket should feature the steps students have discovered plus any illustrations or humor your students wish to add. (Tickets can be large.) Post the tickets in the room.

Close in prayer.

LET'S DON'T EVEN THINK ABOUT ALL THE OTHER THINGS THAT LIVE UNDER WATER LIKE SQUIDS, JELLYFISH AND ELECTRIC EELS. I COULD PUT UP WITH A STARFISH OR TWO. THEY'RE CUTE.

10

NO WORRIES — 99.99 PERCENT OF ALL SEA CREATURES CAN'T LIVE OUT OF WATER. IF YOU PULL THEM OUT, THEY DIE. LAND IS A WORLD THEY CAN'T LIVE IN.

WHEN OUR WORLD — PLANET EARTH — ENDS, THERE WILL BE A LOT OF FISH OUT OF WATER — THE HUMAN KIND. IN LUKE 21:33, JESUS SAYS, "HEAVEN AND EARTH WILL PASS AWAY." (HEAVEN MEANING THE EARTH'S ATMOSPHERE.)

BUT THERE WILL BE A NEW WORLD: "THE HEAVENS WILL DISAPPEAR WITH A ROAR; THE ELEMENTS WILL BE DESTROYED BY FIRE, AND THE EARTH AND EVERYTHING IN IT WILL BE LAID BARE. BUT IN KEEPING WITH HIS PROMISE WE ARE LOOKING FORWARD TO A NEW HEAVEN AND A NEW EARTH, THE HOME OF RIGHTEOUSNESS." (2 PETER 3:10, 13).

11

THE NEW EARTH WILL BE DIFFERENT. IN FACT, IT WILL BE SO COMPLETELY DIFFERENT THAT UNGODLY PEOPLE WILL BE LIKE FISH OUT OF WATER THERE! JESUS SAID, "HE WHO OVERCOMES WILL INHERIT ALL THIS, AND I WILL BE HIS GOD AND HE WILL BE MY SON" (REVELATION 21:7).

"HE WHO OVERCOMES" IS THE CHRISTIAN! FISH WON'T MAKE IT. BUT IT'S GOING TO BE A FUN PLACE FOR YOU AND ME. SEE YOU THERE!

12

THE NEW EARTH WILL BE DIFFERENT. IN FACT, IT WILL BE SO COMPLETELY DIFFERENT THAT UNGODLY PEOPLE WILL BE LIKE **FISH OUT OF WATER** THERE! JESUS SAID, **"HE WHO OVERCOMES WILL INHERIT ALL THIS, AND I WILL BE HIS GOD AND HE WILL BE MY SON"** (REVELATION 21:7).

"HE WHO OVERCOMES" IS THE **CHRISTIAN!** FISH WON'T MAKE IT. BUT IT'S GOING TO BE A FUN PLACE FOR YOU AND ME. SEE YOU THERE!

LET'S DON'T EVEN **THINK** ABOUT ALL THE OTHER THINGS THAT LIVE UNDER WATER LIKE SQUIDS, JELLYFISH AND ELECTRIC EELS. I COULD PUT UP WITH A **STARFISH** OR TWO. THEY'RE CUTE.

LET'S HOPE THIS ISN'T A NEW TREND. IT'S BAD ENOUGH TRYING TO DODGE CATS AND DOGS AND OTHER CARS WHILE DRIVING. I WOULDN'T WANT TO SMASH INTO A **GREY WHALE** ATTEMPTING TO CROSS THE STREET.

WOULD YOU LIKE TO WAKE UP AND FIND YOUR CAR COVERED WITH **BARNACLES**?

I FOR ONE DON'T WANT TO FIND A **LOBSTER** UNDER MY SHEETS.

HAVE YOU HEARD ABOUT THOSE FISH THAT ARE TAKING OVER FLORIDA? SOME STRANGE FISH THAT BREATHE AIR AND WALK ON FINS ARE TRAVELING THE HIGHWAYS AND BYWAYS OF THE SOUTHEAST, FROM POND TO POND.
DISNEY WORLD

2

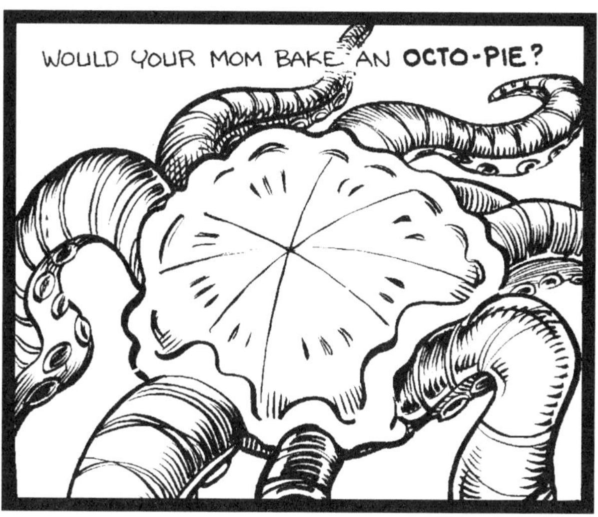

NO WORRIES — 99.99 PERCENT OF ALL SEA CREATURES CAN'T LIVE OUT OF WATER. IF YOU PULL THEM OUT, THEY DIE. LAND IS A WORLD THEY CAN'T LIVE IN.
WHEN OUR WORLD — PLANET EARTH — ENDS, THERE WILL BE A LOT OF FISH OUT OF WATER — THE HUMAN KIND. IN LUKE 21:33, JESUS SAYS, "HEAVEN AND EARTH WILL PASS AWAY." (HEAVEN MEANING THE EARTH'S ATMOSPHERE.)
BUT THERE WILL BE A NEW WORLD: "THE HEAVENS WILL DISAPPEAR WITH A ROAR; THE ELEMENTS WILL BE DESTROYED BY FIRE, AND THE EARTH AND EVERYTHING IN IT WILL BE LAID BARE. BUT IN KEEPING WITH HIS PROMISE WE ARE LOOKING FORWARD TO A NEW HEAVEN AND A NEW EARTH, THE HOME OF RIGHTEOUSNESS" (2 PETER 3:10, 13).

11

AND WHAT IF A KNOCK COMES ON THE DOOR AND A QUIET VOICE SAYS ...
CANDYGRAM.
COULD IT REALLY BE A LAND SHARK WAITING TO BITE OFF YOUR HEAD?

4

WOULD YOUR MOM BAKE AN OCTO-PIE?

9

AND IT'S GROSS ENOUGH SQUASHING THOSE UGLY FAT GREEN CATERPILLERS EATING THE TOMATO PLANTS. CAN YOU IMAGINE STEPPING ON A SEA SLUG?

6

AND WHAT ABOUT SEA SNAILS IN YOUR YARD? THOSE THINGS GROW AS BIG AS TRUCK TIRES.

7

Stay Connected!

Focus of the Lesson: Although God has given us free will, it pays to stay connected to Him.
Biblical Basis: John 15:1-8
Materials Needed: Copies of the "Stay Connected" booklet, chalkboard and chalk, 3x5-inch index cards, a controlled device or a controller (radio controlled model car, TV remote control or the like), paper, pencils.

Step 1—Approach to the Word
Show your class the controlled device or a controller. Pass the object around, if appropriate, and say, **How many of you want to have a great life? This object is going to give us an important hint about how to have a great life. Can you guess what that hint is?** Assure students that they will discover the answer as they jump into the lesson.

Step 2—Bible Exploration
Have students tell what controls these things (list them on the chalkboard):

> Television set (Remote control)
> RC race car (Radio controller)
> Kids (Parents)
> Room lights (Wall switch)
> Football teams (Coaches, referees)
> Lawbreakers (Police, judges, jails)

Ask, **Do you agree or disagree with the statement "All of the things listed should be controlled"?** Ask your students to describe some of the advantages and disadvantages of controlling each one. Your students will probably heavily favor the idea of control in each case. Some students may point out that some forms of control are healthy and positive but some can be abusive and harmful.

Now ask, **Is it good for you to be controlled? Why or why not?** Allow free discussion.

Give each student a copy of the "Stay Connected" booklet. After students have had a chance to read the booklets, ask them to describe the problem with the robot—why did it lose control? (The control line was broken, so the robot lost its connection to the control box.)

Read John 15:1-8. Ask students to report what "control line" they see in this passage. Their answers should center on remaining in Christ (see vv. 5-10). Have students tell if this is a positive, healthy kind of control or a control that stifles and harms. Discuss the role that obedience to God plays in the process of remaining in Him (see v. 10).

Point out that as long as a Christian remains in Christ, a great life can be enjoyed.

Step 3—Life Exploration
Remind students that it is easy to remain in Christ and act like Christians during Bible study time like this, but things can be different out there in the world of temptations. Have students suggest several temptations young people are likely to face.

Have your class form groups of three or four students. Give each group paper and pencils. Assign each group a different temptation. Each group is to write a short skit dealing with that temptation. The skits should show how a person can choose to stay connected to Christ and what happens when a person stays connected or breaks the connection.

Encourage students to make their skits powerful, dealing with emotional issues. Humor is great, too.

Perform the skits and discuss practical ways to remain in Christ.

Step 4—Conclusion
Distribute index cards. Each student is to make a "God Is My Controller" wallet card on which he or she writes a short note or prayer of commitment to remain in Christ.

You and I are not robots. God gave each of us a free will. Even so, it pays to stay "connected" to Jesus! Otherwise, our lives are out of control.

Jesus said, "APART FROM ME YOU CAN DO NOTHING" (John 15:5).

So stay connected.

STAY
Connected!
TOM FINLEY

BOY, WAS THE ROBOT OUT OF CONTROL.
GRIND!
NORTH POLE
PEEL!

I HOOKED UP THE CONTROL BOX AND PUSHED THE POWER BUTTON.
CLICK!

HE SLAM DUNKS IT!
YAY!

JUNIOR SEEMED TO GET THE HANG OF THINGS QUICKLY.
WHAM! WHAM! WHAM!
GOO!

You and I are not robots. God gave each of us a free will. Even so, it pays to stay "connected" to Jesus! Otherwise, our lives are out of control.

Jesus said,

"APART FROM ME YOU CAN DO NOTHING" (John 15:5).

So stay connected.

What Mason Saw

Focus of the Lesson: We need to be aware of obstacles to the Christian's power for daily living.
Biblical Basis: Zechariah 4:6,7
Materials Needed: Copies of the "What Mason Saw" booklet, chalkboard and chalk, plenty of paper, pencils or felt-tip pens, a few staplers. Optional: magazines, scissors, paste.

Step 1—Approach to the Word

Tell your students about the Tournament of Roses parade float that ran out of gas. Grinding to a halt, it blocked the parade until someone could get a can of gas. The silly thing was that this float represented the Standard Oil Company. With its huge supply of gasoline, the Standard Oil float was out of gas.

Point out that Christians have an infinite source of power in God—power for daily living. It often seems that Christians don't experience or use that power. This session talks about things that can disconnect a person from God's power.

Step 2—Bible Exploration

As you read Zechariah 4:6,7 with your class, explain its background. At the time this portion of the Bible was written, the Temple in Jerusalem had been destroyed by enemies. Now it was time to rebuild, a tremendously difficult undertaking. Zerubbabel was one of the leaders charged with the job. Zechariah 4:6,7 records God's encouragement to Zerubbabel.

Say, **Here we see a beautiful image of God assuring His power to a man in need. God promised divine power rather than human might and power. This is the way it would be, even for us. We can have God's power to live our Christian lives to their fullest. But sometimes things can prevent a Christian from enjoying God's power. Let's look at one such thing right now.**

Distribute copies of the "What Mason Saw" booklet. Ask, **What was Mason's problem? How was it solved?** Mason's problem was lack of knowledge. He didn't know about the available power, he didn't know how to tap into it. In the same way, a Christian can miss much of God's power simply because he doesn't know much about it.

Step 3—Life Exploration

Have your class form groups of three or four students. Give each group paper, pencils or felt-tip pens, and staplers to make a booklet called "How to Be a Sickly Weakling." Optional: provide magazines, scissors and paste so students can illustrate their booklets with magazine photos.

Across the top of the chalkboard, write this heading: "If You Want to Be a Sickly Weakling, Avoid These Important Truths...." Under that heading form two columns, one entitled "A Powerful Body," the other "A Powerful Christian." Each column should contain this list: 1. Healthy Exercise; 2. Proper Diet; 3. Good Hygiene; 4. Wise Behavior; 5. Healthy Attitude; 6. Commitment to Excellence.

Explain that you want each group to make a booklet entitled "How to Be a Sickly Weakling." Give these instructions: **Look at the items I've listed on the chalkboard. Create a one- or two-page chapter for each item. Each chapter should include a short paragraph of explanation and a drawing or photo to illustrate the chapter. For example, chapter 1 might be called "At All Costs, Avoid Proper Exercise." Describe healthy exercise as it applies to a bodybuilder and as it applies to a Christian. Examples of healthy Christian exercise are prayer, fellowship and talking about God. Have fun with these but be sure they cover each subject properly.**

This is a complex project, so walk from group to group offering advice and helping kids think of examples of things that, if avoided, weaken a Christian. You may wish to encourage a classroom-wide discussion as each group works, to allow for a free exchange of insights and ideas.

When everyone is finished, discuss what students have come up with.

Step 4—Conclusion

Encourage students to habitually practice the things that make for a powerful Christian life.

"'NOT BY MIGHT NOR BY POWER, BUT BY MY SPIRIT' SAYS THE LORD ALMIGHTY" (ZECHARIAH 4:6).

THIS VERSE FROM THE OLD TESTAMENT TELLS US THAT REAL STRENGTH COMES NOT FROM HUMAN MIGHT OR POWER, BUT FROM GOD!

MASON DIDN'T KNOW ABOUT THE POWER AT HIS COMMAND. AS A CHRISTIAN, YOU CAN TAP INTO GOD'S POWER FOR DAILY LIVING THROUGH HIS HOLY SPIRIT!

What Mason Saw
Tom Finley

VA-ROOM!
START IT UP?

THIS THING WILL CUT THROUGH ANY WOOD YOU GOT LIKE A KNIFE THROUGH WARM BUTTER.

IT TOOK ME ALL DAY TO CUT DOWN ONE TREE!

BUT...
WARM BUTTER? I'VE BEEN LIED TO!!

2

"'NOT BY MIGHT NOR BY POWER, BUT BY MY SPIRIT' SAYS THE LORD ALMIGHTY" (ZECHARIAH 4:6).

THIS VERSE FROM THE OLD TESTAMENT TELLS US THAT REAL STRENGTH COMES NOT FROM HUMAN MIGHT OR POWER, BUT FROM GOD!

MASON DIDN'T KNOW ABOUT THE POWER AT HIS COMMAND. AS A CHRISTIAN, YOU CAN TAP INTO GOD'S POWER FOR DAILY LIVING THROUGH HIS HOLY SPIRIT!

11

4

9

6

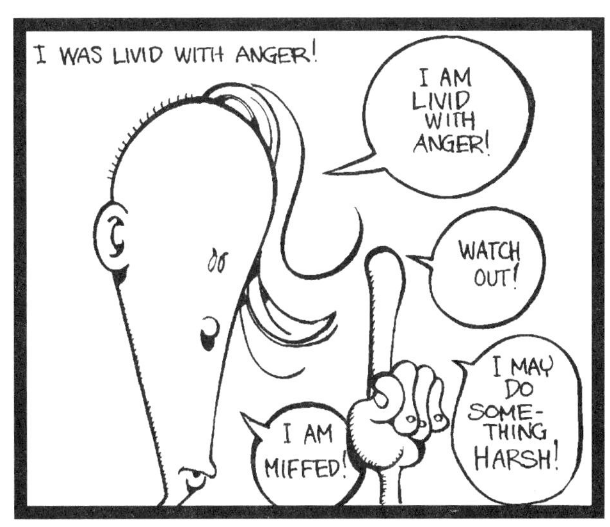

7

The Wisdom Formula ®

Focus of the Lesson: God oversaw the process of how the Bible came to be.
Biblical Basis: Proverbs 2:6; 2 Timothy 3:16
Materials Needed: Copies of "The Wisdom Formula" booklet, chalkboard and chalk, paper, pencils, supplies for making a large poster, a Bible trivia game as described in the Conclusion section.
Before Class: Arrange a demonstration as described in the second paragraph of Step 2. You'll need a biblically knowledgeable adult if you wish to do the alternative suggestion in the Life Exploration section.

Step 1—Approach to the Word

Give a copy of "The Wisdom Formula" booklet to each student to read. Discuss the significance of the verse quoted on page 10—Proverbs 2:6.

Ask, **Have you ever wondered how this incredibly important Book we call the Bible went from its beginnings centuries ago in far-off places to the Books we now hold in our hands? Today we are going to find out how we got this great source of wisdom, knowledge and understanding.**

Step 2—Bible Exploration

On the chalkboard draw five columns. Head the columns with these phrases: A. Inspiration and Writing; B. Circulation; C. Copies Made and Distributed; D. Books Collected and Canonized; E. Translation Based on Best Copies Available.

Before class, arrange to have someone from outside the group run into your classroom at your signal, shout "hallelujah" seven times and run out again in the wink of an eye. You will ask students to silently list on paper the answers to several questions.

As soon as the person leaves the classroom, give students paper and pencils. Ask questions about what was shouted (and how many times), the color of the person's eyes, the color of the person's shoes and other clothing articles, the presence or absence of a watch, jewelry, belt and so on.

Call for answers to be read from the students' lists. Your actor can return for this. Did anyone have all the correct answers? Probably not.

Explain that your students were witnesses to a simple event. The trouble is, it's hard to be 100 percent accurate. The people who wrote the various portions of the Bible were also witnesses, mere humans like us. But we claim there is no error in the original writings. How did fallible humans write infallible truth? Point to column A on the board. Read and discuss 2 Timothy 3:16. It says that God breathed (inspired) the Scriptures. He made sure they got it right.

The original writings were then circulated. The New Testament letters, for instance, were sent from church to church to be read aloud. As often as possible, copies were made as the letters passed through. Copies of copies were made until many hundreds existed.

Early on it became illegal to own copies of the New Testament writings because Christianity was declared illegal by the Romans. Anyone caught with such a writing was jailed, or more likely, killed. The trouble was, there were many writings in circulation written by many Christians. Some of these were of questionable origins containing truth, perhaps, but not God-breathed. Were these worth dying for? So the next step in Bible history was to decide which were actually inspired, sacred writings and which were not. Councils of church leaders met to decide the issue and the contents of the Bible as we know it came to be. That process is called "canonization."

Finally, translations into other languages were made. The best translations are those based on the best copies—due to copying errors, some copies are slightly different than others. However, no difference is great enough to cause big trouble.

Step 3—Life Exploration

Have your class form groups of three or four students. Have each group make a section of a poster that forms the process of how our Bible came to be. For example, one group could work on the first column, drawing a cartoon of someone writing on a scroll as God peers down from a cloud. Tape the various completed sections together and display.

As an alternative to the poster, call in your minister or other biblically knowledgeable adult to comment on the Bible and answer questions.

Step 4—Conclusion

After once again emphasizing the importance of the Bible to the daily life of each believer, play a simple Bible trivia game for fun. (Someone in your church undoubtedly has such a game.) Or think up 15 or more questions about the Bible (how many books in the Bible, how many apostles, who was the oldest man in the Bible and so on).

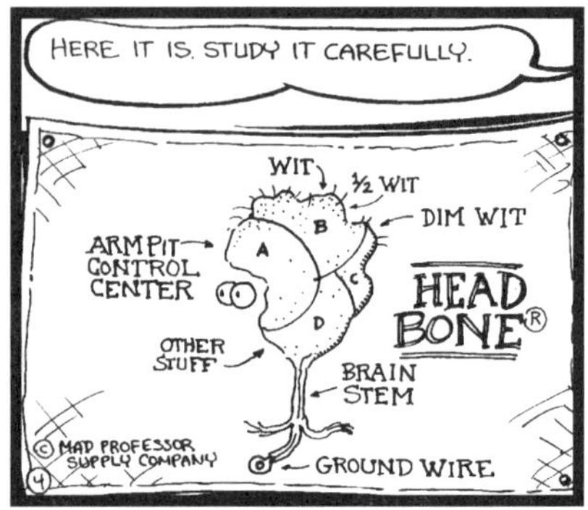

THE PROFESSOR LEARNED WISDOM DOESN'T COME IN A BOTTLE.

So, IF YOU WANT TO BE A WISE PERSON, WHERE **DO** YOU FIND WISDOM? IN THE <u>BIBLE</u>!

"FOR THE LORD GIVES **WISDOM**, AND FROM HIS MOUTH COME **KNOWLEDGE** AND **UNDER-STANDING**" (PROVERBS 2:6).

HIS WORDS ARE IN THE BOOK. READ IT!!!

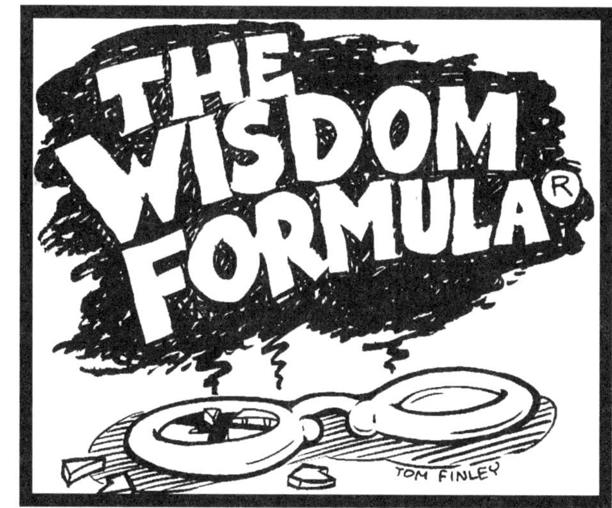

THE PROFESSOR LEARNED WISDOM DOESN'T COME IN A BOTTLE.
SO, IF YOU WANT TO BE A WISE PERSON, WHERE **DO** YOU FIND WISDOM? IN THE <u>BIBLE</u>!

"FOR THE LORD GIVES **WISDOM**, AND FROM HIS MOUTH COME **KNOWLEDGE** AND **UNDER-STANDING**" (PROVERBS 2:6).

HIS WORDS ARE IN THE BOOK. READ IT!!!

PROFESSOR E. EMSIE SQUARE HERE, THE WORLD'S MOST VERY GREATEST SCIENTIFIC GENIUS! I HAVE INVENTED A TOP-SECRET WISDOM FORMULA®!

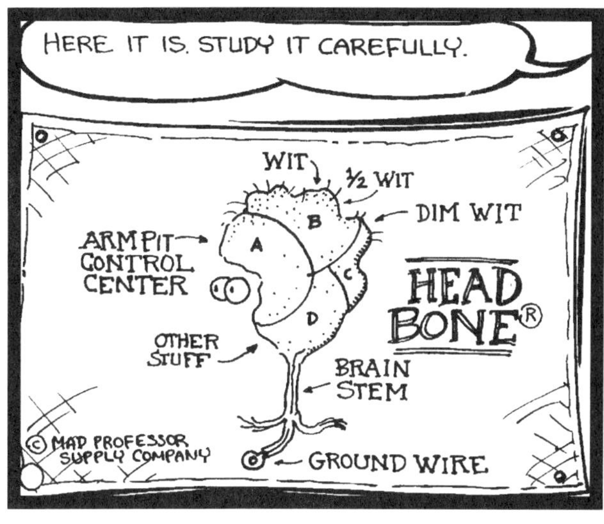

HERE IT IS. STUDY IT CAREFULLY.
WIT
½ WIT
DIM WIT
ARMPIT CONTROL CENTER
A
B
C
D
HEAD BONE®
OTHER STUFF
BRAIN STEM
© MAD PROFESSOR SUPPLY COMPANY
GROUND WIRE

DEAR READER—
WE REGRET TO INFORM YOU THAT PROFESSOR E. EMSIE SQUARE CAN NO LONGER APPEAR IN THIS PUBLICATION.
THANK YOU.

WATCH AS I MIX IT UP... ♫ HUM-DE-DUM... ♪
♫ HUM... ARE YOU READY FOR SOME FOOTBALL?!?♪ ♫ HUM-DE-DUH...

AND HERE WE GO! THIS IS MY TOP SECRET WISDOM FORMULA®! ONE SWALLOW OF THIS AND I, PROFESSOR E. EMSIE SQUARE, SHALL BECOME THE WISEST PERSON ON EARTH! I SHALL RULE THE WORLD!! YOU'LL ALL BE MY SLAVES!
HAARRRR!